HOT. PASSIONATE.
AND *ILLEGAL?*

HOT. PASSIONATE. AND ILLEGAL?

Why (Almost) Everything You
Thought About Latinos Just May Be True

CRISTIÁN DE LA FUENTE
AND
FEDERICO LARIÑO

A CELEBRA BOOK

CELEBRA
Published by New American Library, a division of
Penguin Group (USA) Inc., 375 Hudson Street,
New York, New York 10014, USA
Penguin Group (Canada), 90 Eglinton Avenue East, Suite 700, Toronto,
Ontario M4P 2Y3, Canada (a division of Pearson Penguin Canada Inc.)
Penguin Books Ltd., 80 Strand, London WC2R 0RL, England
Penguin Ireland, 25 St. Stephen's Green, Dublin 2,
Ireland (a division of Penguin Books Ltd.)
Penguin Group (Australia), 250 Camberwell Road, Camberwell, Victoria 3124,
Australia (a division of Pearson Australia Group Pty. Ltd.)
Penguin Books India Pvt. Ltd., 11 Community Centre, Panchsheel Park, New Delhi - 110
017, India
Penguin Group (NZ), 67 Apollo Drive, Rosedale, North Shore 0632,
New Zealand (a division of Pearson New Zealand Ltd.)
Penguin Books (South Africa) (Pty.) Ltd., 24 Sturdee Avenue,
Rosebank, Johannesburg 2196, South Africa

Penguin Books Ltd., Registered Offices:
80 Strand, London WC2R 0RL, England

First published by Celebra,
a division of Penguin Group (USA) Inc.

First Printing, January 2010
10 9 8 7 6 5 4 3 2 1

Copyright © DLF, Inc., 2010
All rights reserved

CELEBRA and logo are trademarks of Penguin Group (USA) Inc.

Library of Congress Cataloging-in-Publication Data:

Fuente, Cristián de la, 1974—
    Hot. passionate. and illegal?:why (almost) everything you thought about Latinos just may be
true/Cristián de la Fuente and Federico Lariño.
    p.   cm.
    "A Celebra Book."
    ISBN 978-0-451-22804-8
    1. Hispanic Americans.   2. Hispanic Americans—Social life and customs.   3. Stereotypes
(Social psychology)   I. Lariño, Federico.   II. Title.
    E184.S75F84 2010
    973'.0468—dc22   2009029560

Set in Adobe Caslon
Designed by Spring Hoteling

Printed in the United States of America

HUMBOLDT PARK

To my mom and dad, who met in Chile, dated and conceived me in Miami. To my wife, who was born in Chile and didn't want to date me there until we found each other in Los Angeles and finally got married in Chile. And to the love of my life, my daughter, Laura, who was born in Miami, lives in Los Angeles, and thinks she's Chilean. This book is for you.

—Cristián de la Fuente

This book is dedicated to Coque, my grandfather, who lived all of his life in Argentina. To Mariela, my wife, who was born in the United States. To Santiago, my son, who was born in Argentina and immigrated with us. And to Tamara, my daughter, who was born in the United States after we immigrated. I dare you to try to understand this Latino family.

—Federico Lariño

ACKNOWLEDGMENTS

Gracias to my dad and mom, for teaching me that everything is possible. Gracias to Univision, Ray, Alina, Otto, Cisco and Mario, for developing a late-night show that allowed me to meet Federico. Gracias to Luis Balaguer and Conchita Oliva for making that deal. A special note of appreciation to our friends at Penguin, Raymond Garcia, Mark Chait and Kim Suarez, who worked so hard by our side to make this book possible. Also gracias to Jeremie Ruby-Strauss for helping us trim the fat of this fine piece of literature. Gracias to Stephen Espinoza for not being only my attorney, and the best one, but my friend. Gracias to Harry Abrams, Marni Rosenzweig, Joe Rice, Alec Shankman and everybody at Abrams for believing in me and turning this idea into a book. Gracias to Cynthia Snyder for planning my life. Gracias to Deena Katz and everybody at DWTS. Gracias to David Maples for creating Raph, the first Latino role with an accent. Gracias to my bank that lent me money when I didn't have any. Gracias to everybody that is not mentioned because I haven't met you yet or because I forgot and I'll apologize later.

—Cristián de la Fuente

I'd like to extend my gracias to all of the above—except for Cristián's Bank. In addition, I'd like to send my love to Ninin,

Otye and Matías for always being there. A personal note of thanks to Carlos de Urquiza, Juan Carlos Mastrángelo, Paul Bouche and Daniel Gutman for having taught me priceless lessons, sometimes without having been aware of it. I am grateful to Victor Agu, Fernando Balmayor, Gonzalo Morozzi, the Culotta family and the Pirogovsky family, because everybody needs people like them in their lives. Special thanks to David Barski, Cisco Suarez and Maria Lopez Alvarez, for always believing in me.

—Federico Lariño

And, finally, our special heartfelt thanks to all the Latino immigrants living in the United States. We tend to think that this book took thirty years to complete, because it has the knowledge and experiences of most of the Latinos who have immigrated throughout those years. Our last gracias goes to all the Michael Gonzalezes and Taylor Perezes around us.

TABLE OF CONTENTS

PART 2
CULTURE AND PEOPLE

PART 3
LANGUAGE AND MEDIA

PART 4
WORK AND POLITICS

HOT. PASSIONATE.
AND ILLEGAL?

PREFACE

WHO AM I, AND WHY ARE YOU READING THIS?

I am from Chile.

No, that's not a typo. There is a South American country called Chile, and I'm from there. Some people are confused by this, because chile (sometimes spelled chili or chilli) can mean a type of pepper, a sauce, or even a bowl of spicy meat and beans. I can assure you my home country is none of these things. I used to feel insulted when people thought I was claiming to be not only a vegetable but one that causes tears, especially because some of my ex-girlfriends have made similar accusations. I stopped getting offended when I saw that this running joke has God's personal approval—Chile, the country, is in fact shaped like a chili pepper. At first I denied it, but I've since given in. I know when I've been beaten.

I'm also an actor. I'm very proud to have broken into Hollywood as a Latino. It can be very difficult when every character they'll audition you for is a drug dealer, pimp, or smuggler. Sometimes you'll get something like a male nurse, and you think, "Okay, it's not a doctor, but still not too bad." When you go to the audition, you look at the "sides," which are basically one or two scenes containing your lines. You read for it, and hey, you get the part! That's when they give you the rest of the script, and you see that your ex-smuggler nurse character has sworn off dealing, but he does do a little pimping on the side to cover his bets on illegal cockfighting. Once you make peace with all of this and somehow rationalize that your character is doing what he has to do in a complex world, they kill him off in the first five minutes of the movie. Before you can get angry about it, the director decides to cut your scene entirely. But what matters is you've done it, you've given life to the best parking valet an audience could ever dream of! (Okay, it's not much, but it beats waiting tables.)

I was incredibly lucky in that I landed my first big role alongside a major star just two years after I moved to the United States. I played a car racer named Memo Moreno in the movie *Driven* with Sylvester Stallone. I was so happy. There was just one nagging detail that concerned me. Memo's background said he was from Brazil. As you know, I'm from Chile. I asked around, does this not bother anyone? "Why should it?" they would ask. Ah, let's see, they don't even speak Spanish in Brazil? People looked at me like I had two heads. *What are you talking about, and who really cares?*

It's a mixed blessing for Latino actors that to the Anglos in this country, all of our accents sound the same. You can play a Mexican, Cuban, Puerto Rican, Brazilian, whatever. Just don't be stupid and make a fuss about it, like I almost did. Instead, make sure you have a thick skin and *quietly cash the check*: nothing to see here.

Years later, at the very beginning of my journey on *Dancing with the Stars*, I had my first meeting with the producers. As soon as they saw me walk into the room, one of them said, "Why are you not dancing?" I looked around. There was no music playing.

"I'm sorry, did I miss my cue?" I had no clue what they were talking about.

They all laughed, and they explained, "You are Latino. We thought you'd dance right in to the meeting!" I was shocked at the stereotypes and misconceptions people in this country have about us. Just then, I made a silent vow. I would show millions of Americans that each of us defies easy categorization. Everyone is different, complex, and unique. I would teach them these things by publicly showcasing a pure, simple, and undeniable truth: I have no innate dancing ability whatsoever.

Looking back, this experience is what really got me thinking, and it led me down the path of writing this book. America just didn't know very much about people like me. I realized that in order for people to really know and understand us, they first need to understand where we come from. They need to understand *Latinos.*

Who are your new neighbors? you ask. Who is this group with whom you've ended up sharing your land, thanks in part to your own use of the slogan "the land of opportunity" within earshot of various declining economies? Fear not, I am here to help. I will tell you everything you need to know.

Let me now address my Latino readers. I understand you may initially feel alarmed that I am sharing too much confidential information. We must reject this kind of thinking. From understanding comes a more peaceful coexistence, and the more we learn about each other, the better for all of us. Plus, of course I'm not going to share the really *secret* stuff, don't be insane.

Currently, minorities make up about one-third of the total population of the United States. Experts predict that within approximately forty years there will be more minorities than Anglo people living in this country. In particular, the Hispanic population is projected to nearly triple between now and the year

2050, by which time nearly one in three U.S. residents will be Latino. I know, it's hard to believe.

So that's the picture of where we're headed. Increasingly, you are going to be living with, working with, and depending upon Latino doctors, teachers, and lawyers in your everyday life. Your next-door neighbor could be a Latino doctor. Your son's teacher could be Latina. As soon as your Latino doctor prescribes the wrong medication to your mother or your son tries to kiss the Latina teacher, you will need none other than your Latino lawyer. My point is that you want Latinos to be your friends, to be on your side. I can't emphasize this enough: We are the *number one minority in this country*. Given what lies ahead for all of us, what better time than now to really get to know and understand each other?

But Cristián, what about those of us who bought your book for other reasons?

How could I forget you? I couldn't. When people first heard that I was writing this book, a lot of them said, "Oh, that makes sense, he's so handsome." I would like to be clear on this. I don't refuse or deny my looks, but what does that have to do with anything? However, I went ahead and put my face on the cover. I hope I have made you satisfied with your purchase. If, on the other hand, you thought this would be a book of traditional Latino recipes, I will add some of my mother's best dishes, just in case. Finally, if you recognized my name as an actor and thought this book would be a tell-all of Hollywood's dirtiest gossip, please let someone at the bookstore know they are putting my book in the wrong section (unless it is in the front; then it can stay). In any case, I hope you enjoy reading my book as much as I enjoyed smiling for the cover photo, which I did with such enthusiasm that my face ached the next day.

CRISTIÁN DE LA FUENTE

PS: Yes, I'm the Latino guy who made it to the finals on the sixth season of *Dancing with the Stars.*

PPS: Yes, my arm injury was real.

PPPS: I'm fully recovered now. Thank you for your kindness.

PART 1

WHO WE ARE: THE BASICS

CHAPTER 1

"LATINO" OR "HISPANIC"?

I have good news and bad news. The good news is that we just started an exciting journey together, and now we are on the road to knowledge. The bad news is that an angry mob has set our car on fire and so we are hitchhiking.

If you want to get to know somebody, the first thing you have to learn is what he'd like to be called. What's the correct term for a person from a Latin American country? Is it "Latino," "Hispanic," "Latin," "Mexican," "Spanish," or what?

Myth: We hate to be referred to as Hispanics.

Truth: The term "Hispanic" is often used interchangeably with the term "Latino."

The only wrong answers are "Mexican," unless the person is from Mexico, of course, and "Spanish," because Spain is not a Latin American country.

The U.S. government introduced the term "Hispanic" into the 1970 census, as a way to identify all immigrants who came from, or who had parents who came from, Spanish-speaking countries, regardless of race. The 1970s were a different time, and I guess if your boss just got back from a four-martini lunch, he didn't notice that you called a quickly increasing population of minorities "his-panic." Or else he did notice and thinks it's hilarious.

"Latino" refers to the Latin American origins of many of this group's members, and it was officially adopted in 1997 by the U.S. government as a synonym for the term "Hispanic." Neither one of them refers to a race, because a Latino or Hispanic person can be of any race. "Latino" has become the more popular term in the United States, but neither should be thought of as offensive. Unfortunately, that doesn't mean a lot of Latinos/Hispanics don't feel strongly about which ethnic label they prefer. Then you've got the Latin Grammy Awards, in which I didn't hear one word of Latin, so even I get confused. Kids always have the best answers, so the other day I asked my daughter: "How do *you* like to be called?" and she answered, "Laura."

It is a funny truth that the more mistaken a word is, the more popular and accepted it becomes. Christopher Columbus thought he had landed in India when he stumbled upon the Americas, and to this day Native Americans are called Indians. Instead of the black pepper he sought, he found chilis, but he called them peppers anyway, and now so does everyone else. In that grand tradition, I am going to use "Latinos" throughout this book, even though Julius Caesar wouldn't understand one word of *Sábado Gigante*. To all the self-described "Hispanics" who are offended by this unilateral decision, by all means: Go back to Spain.

Look how quickly we've already taken a first step toward greater clarity. We've settled on the term "Latinos" to describe the U.S. Spanish-speaking population that migrated from Latin American countries, or our descendants, not because it's necessarily more correct, but because it's the more current label. However, just as we do this, reality intervenes to make the issue fuzzy again. A group of people I call Limbo Latinos introduce a new level of complexity to the puzzle. Let's see if you recognize any of your Latino acquaintances here:

CASE #1: THE CHAMELEON.

A Latino arrives in the United States, the land of opportunity. He's full of hope, but he thinks that the only way to make it in a country so different from the one he was born in is to assimilate into the new society. His passport reads "Felipe Sanchez," but he'll translate it on his driver's license to "Philip." This is where you get your Tyler Gutierrez, your Cody Garcia, and your Nigel Lopez. Despite having lived only six months in the United States, when he calls his family back in his home country, he will throw in some English words, as if he were forgetting his Spanish. This individual doesn't care whether you call him Hispanic or Latino, as long as you do it *privately*.

CASE #2: THE THIRD GENERATION.

He is a grandson of immigrants. His father was born in the United States, as was his mother, his sister, his brother, and his dog. He doesn't speak Spanish, because he hears English all day at school and it's spoken by all his friends, and Spanish he hears only from his grandma. Although he has nothing linking himself to Latinos besides genes and having *arroz con frijoles* for lunch twice a week, his driver's license reads "Rolando Torreño de Garcia." If somebody asks him his nationality, he says: "Nuyorican."

These Limbo Latinos don't get the full Latino experience of immigrants or our children, but they'll never be 100 percent Americans, either. If eating a country's food is enough reason to claim yourself as a citizen of that country, then, you know, I'm Thai.

CASE #3: THE REVERSED CROSSOVER.

This is usually the fourth generation. His parents have no Latino customs whatsoever, no Spanish, not a single trip to the old country, nothing. Even more, they don't know anybody back there. They don't seem like Latinos, because they no longer are. However, he desperately wants to be recognized as "Latino." Why? Because being "American" used to be the only thing that sold, but being "Latino" in the twenty-first century sells, too. He dusts off Grandpa's portrait and stakes this claim.

Christina Aguilera, who sings in Spanish by phonetics, sells millions of records to Latinos; meanwhile, she needs a translator for the Hispanic media interviews because she doesn't have a clue what they're saying to her. At least Cameron Diaz, whose father is Emilio Diaz, Cuban-born, does not try to star in Spanish-spoken movies or to shout phrases like "Death to Fidel Castro!" while schmoozing at the Oscars. If these kinds of things continue to happen, we'll end up seeing people as white as Conan O'Brien wearing guayaberas, dancing salsa, and saying, "Oie, I'm Latino de alma, brother!"

CHAPTER 2

Learn How to Differentiate Latinos in the United States

Let's start at the beginning: Latinos aren't all the same. Latino people don't migrate from a single country, but from a bunch of distinct lands. And the people in those lands, in turn, came from a bunch of other distinct lands. We come in more colors, shapes, and sizes than Angelina Jolie could ever adopt. Our countries of origin have a lot in common, yet thousands of little details distinguish them. If you, my Anglo reader, can manage to correctly identify them, you're going to see an improvement in your relationship with the group, without a doubt.

The majority of Latinos in the United States are Mexicans, thanks to the fact that the countries border each other and that a big chunk of the United States *was* Mexico until 1848.

The top five Latino groups by specific origin:

Mexicans: 28,339,000 (64.0%)

Puerto Ricans: 3,988,000 (9.0%)

Cubans: 1,520,000 (3.4%)

Salvadorans: 1,372,000 (3.1%)

Dominicans: 1,217,000 (2.8 %)

Source: U.S. Census Bureau, 2006 American Community Survey

I'm going to use an example of how to differentiate Latinos based on our countries of origin. It's Monday morning. Beautiful day. You arrive early at the office and you hear that they've hired a new employee. He's in the office right next to you. On the door, the name reads: Fernando Balmayor. It seems Hispanic. You knock and, while you wait, you try to repeat his name a couple of times in your mind to learn how to pronounce it correctly. He opens the door. "Hi, *Furrnanhdou*, I'd like to introduce myself. I'm John, from Accounting!"

From that point on, your goal is to get to know him. You try to stir up some conversation and be congenial, but in order to get to the next level, you need to know where is he from. You get the sense that it's not polite to come right out and ask, because no one asked what you "were" when you started your job. Some of the following clues could come in handy.

CLUE #1: THE TEMPERATURE.

Does your coworker wear shorts in a snowstorm, while enjoying a Popsicle? If so, he's probably from South America, maybe even Chile. You see, God wasn't done with the puns when he made Chile shaped like a chili. He also made it very chilly. It must have been particularly slow in heaven that day.

CLUE #2: THE HEIGHT.

If your coworker has to tiptoe in order to reach the fifteenth-floor elevator button, there is a good chance that he's Brazilian, Mexican, or Peruvian. While the average height of an Argentinean man is five feet eight and a half inches and a Colombian is over five feet seven, Brazilians average a little over five feet six, Mexicans average just under five feet six, and Peruvians measure in at just under five feet five. Remember, though, good things can come in small packages!

CLUE #3: THE "RUMBA."

Get a CD of salsa music and, acting casually, put the CD in your computer and slowly turn up the volume. Inconspicuously look over at your coworker. If he's, say, Central American, he'll keep working or doing whatever he was doing. But if suddenly he leaps up and shakes his hips like a holy roller, flips his tie over his shoulder and raises his arms in the air in front of everyone in Accounts Receivable, this specimen is Caribbean. A Caribbean Latino wouldn't resist the temptation of salsa dancing, it's in his blood. My theory about dancing is that the warmer the country, the more and better its people dance. Have you ever seen a Cuban, Puerto Rican, Brazilian, Venezuelan, or Colombian who is not a good dancer? I haven't. And in those countries, it's always hot. In my native country, Chile, on the other hand, it's always chilly!

CLUE #4: THE WOMEN.

Every Latino man loves women, even the gay ones, no matter what country we're from; and if she's another man's woman, even better. It's one of the things that unite us, so bringing your sister by the office isn't going to tell you anything except that you made a big mistake. As discussed, we Chileans are not known much for our dancing. Do we just leave the hot Latin-lover title to men from other countries? No, we grow excellent wines that make women *think* we are great dancers!

CLUE #5: THE INS TECHNIQUE.

If nothing else works, make a casual point about your last job as an immigration advisor, and how you know every rule, law, amendment, and option ever written about the topic. Drop the subject and head back to your desk. In less than ten minutes, your Latino coworker will be standing in front of you, bringing up a personal issue, or a relative's, or a close friend's, or an acquaintance's. You won't have to worry about asking his nationality, because he'll be over-sharing every piece of information about his native country and the time and circumstances under which he first entered the United States, showing you photos of his pet, inviting you over for dinner, and offering you the role of godfather of his next-born child.

Once you know your new friend's country of origin, you can Google it and then wow him with your knowledge of all the little things that make his culture distinct among the other Latino cultures. He'll come to see that you're different from all the other Anglos in the office. While he can't normally tell all the Anglos apart, he's going to make a special effort with *you*. Nicely done!

CHAPTER 3

"Macho Man" and Feminism Among Latinos

"Big boys don't cry!" Pepito's father said with a harsh voice. "Big boys don't cry!" echoed Pepito's grandfather. Pepito knew they were right, especially now that he's turned sixteen. But that didn't make it any easier when his younger sister refused to share her dolls.

Myth #1: All male Latinos are *machos*.
Truth is, to be and act like a "macho" is a heavy weight for any man; it is a duty we receive as soon as we're born. Within the male Latino world, you have only two options:

1. You are a *macho*,
or
2. You are not male.

There are no gray zones here. How can it be so extreme? Let me throw in a recent personal experience.

I've never had problems with any of my computers, until I

decided to write this book. As Murphy's Law states: "If anything can go wrong, it will." My computer didn't like to wait for inspiration to come, so it decided to shut itself down for good, like a virtual writers' strike. To make a long story short, I ended up using my wife's computer, a laptop . . . with a *pink cover*. That's okay when you are home, but right now I am on a plane going back to L.A. after attending an event in North Carolina, and I brought her laptop . . . waiting for the inspiration.

Inspiration didn't come when I was in my hotel room, by myself. However, as soon as I got on the plane . . . it hit me. This is one of those times that I thank God for letting me live here in the United States, because nobody on the plane cared that I had a pink computer. This may sound shallow to some, but let me tell you, it represents a crystal-clear dividing line between Anglos and Latinos. Had I been in a public place in Chile with a pink laptop, everybody would be yelling "*maricón*," which is a not-very-nice thing to call gay people. In many Latin American countries, you are labeled as gay just because of little details—for example, if they find you kissing another man. What do they know? You could have been doing research for a role . . . just in case you ever decide to become an actor. You could have been conveying the story line of *Brokeback Mountain*. I don't want to lose the focus here, but the thing is that, at least in Chile, when you have a pink Mac, you are *maricón*. In that kind of environment, I couldn't have used my pink computer to write about pink computers, and you would have been robbed of this chapter.

Myth #2: All machos are Latin lovers.

When I was filming *Driven* with Sylvester Stallone, there was this love scene where Til Schweiger had to kiss Estella Warren, and he couldn't get it right, it wasn't believable. After a lot of takes, Sly got up and said to him, "That's why they call it Latin lovers, you

Cristián de la Fuente

As you can see, not only German actors can play soldiers. The advantage for Latino actors is that we can play the Latin lover, but we can also play the prick. How do we do it? We imagine that we are Germans.

see? You are German, the only good films you can do are war movies, and even in those you end up as losers. You need the Latino blood in your veins to be a Latin lover. Cristián! Come over here and show Til how to do it!" I did it, took a bow, and went back to my seat as if it were the most natural thing to be asked to do.

The thing is that after decades of different myths about Latino manhood, these two main myths (macho and Latin lover) have melted into a single one. These days, a macho Latino has to uphold way too many titles. Not crying is not enough. You have to be a Latin lover, you ought to have money to support your family, and you have to be stronger than normal men. You can't allow yourself to be sad or depressed even for one day. At the house, besides being a good father and husband, you have to be a carpenter, a plumber, a mechanic, and an electrician. In other words, the same four jobs you hold down to make your living outside the home. The macho Latino can't be tired without being labeled as useless and lazy. And I hope you didn't think being a Latin lover meant you get to be a playboy. Sadly, no. This brings us to our first macho truth.

Macho Truth #1: An adult macho is always married.
He doesn't necessarily spend too much time with his wife—that wouldn't be macho. He may love or hate his wife, but he will only show one thing in public: indifference. On some level he might wish he was a playboy, but how could it be? Would he do his own cooking and shopping? Would he wash his own laundry and flip through catalogs, picking out the decorations for his home? It would put him on macho-probation even to ponder these questions.

Macho Truth #2: A macho loves to be noticed.
The macho Latino uses sleeveless, skintight T-shirts to show his muscles. At the same time, machos always speak loud. Every word has to be delivered by yelling in a deep voice, even for the most trivial issues, such as, "Would you please pass the salt!" That is how you get fear and respect from your cousins at the dinner table.

Macho Truth #3: A macho smells like sweat.
Taking a bath is not a macho thing to do, because you end up smelling like soap and shampoo. A spring-fresh macho is not a macho. If, someday, a leading supplier of bath and body products comes up with a soap that smells like axle grease and beef, we could talk again about machos and bathing. In addition, machos don't shave every morning, though they don't let their beards grow too long, either. It's like they are showing the world that while they can dominate their mighty whiskers—even *they* can't do it completely.

Macho Truth #4: Machos don't buy their clothes.

Of course they don't; shopping is a female activity. The macho wives do it on their behalf. The fabric their women choose for them has to have good strength and be resistant, like a construction worker's uniform, but also be appropriate for a wedding or funeral. That's macho clothing. If there's a hole in the clothes, the wife should sew it rather than buy a new one, because each mended tear is a war medal.

Macho Truth #5: Machos fart and burp no matter where they are.

They could be at a job interview, in church, or having sex with their wives. Just as dogs pee to mark their territory, a macho's gas serves as a claim of ownership and a warning to other machos.

Macho Truth #6: A real macho can't stand unmacho men.

A macho only gathers together with other like-minded machos, with whom he spends the whole time arguing about who's more macho. Once among his peers, a macho is expected to make incredible claims concerning his sexual stamina, earning ability, tolerance for hot foods, hemorrhoid severity, maximum bench weight, and how long he's able to hold his breath underwater. The macho is number one, whatever the challenge, like a superhero. As illogical as it might seem, after any given macho gathering, each and every one of them will go back home believing he's the top dog.

Macho Truth #7: There are no "green" machos.

A macho doesn't want to understand saving the planet, living a green life, saving the whales, recycling, or being nice to the environment. A macho thinks about the most extreme ways to waste all the natural resources that he can. High-efficiency lightbulbs? Lightbulbs should smoke and burn your hands when you touch them.

Macho Truth #8: You can't separate a macho from his car.

A macho needs a huge, loud, dirty, gas-guzzling truck. You will never, ever see a macho behind the wheel of a hybrid car. He could live in a small house, but he could never drive a small car. If he could afford an eighteen-wheeler, he'd drive it to his son's Little League games.

When a macho gets in a car, he is always the driver. It doesn't matter if this is a nonstop family trip between San Francisco and New York and he's been driving sixty-nine hours straight, a macho will never allow anybody—especially his wife—to take the wheel. Machos think they should still be the driver even when they are drunk, which according to them, they have never

Cristián de la Fuente

A real macho doesn't care what everybody thinks. If he feels like peeing, he pees. If he feels like yelling, he yells. On this day, in Chile, I felt like washing my hair in public.

been. If you see a woman driving a car with a man in the passenger seat, he's either been blinded in an industrial accident and she's rushing him to the hospital or else you've mistaken a boyish-looking woman for a man.

Macho Truth #9: To a macho, every woman is sexy.
From the teenaged neighbor to his best friend's grandma, this is one of the macho's few virtues: he doesn't discriminate. A girl might be skinny or fat, a sour-faced teetotaler or a sloppy drunk, morally loose or high-strung and shrill, single or married, friendly or mean as a snake—a macho Latino would want to take her to bed as long as she's a woman. And in some cases, with enough makeup, he could make an exception even to that.

If these nine indicators are still not enough for you to establish if the Latino you're studying is truly a macho, try asking him the following questions:

1. Do you know the price of a dozen roses?

2. What's your plan for the next Valentine's Day?

3. What's the last thing your wife said?

If he actually knows the answer to any of them, he's definitely *not* a macho.

FEMINISM WITHIN THE LATINO WORLD.

Latina feminists can be difficult to identify. Being a feminist when you're unmarried and you decide every step of your life is one thing, but it can be trickier when you are part of a large, multigenerational family. For many Latina family women, "independence" is living with her husband and eight children in a different house than her parents. Our tradition is that men and women need each other. The macho is able to be macho because he has a woman washing his clothes, taking care of his kids, running the household, and doing her best to keep the family going. On the other hand, the macho grants the woman the family life she's always dreamed about, allowing her total ownership over the areas she cares about, while handling all the things she thinks are a man's job. In that sense, I believe there's as much or more feedback and synergy between Latino men and women than in any other culture. Let's try to clear up some of the myths about the relationship between Latino men and women:

1. Latino men don't harbor anger toward all women, just the married ones.

2. Latino husbands are not unfaithful by nature, but they don't mind if wifely duties are delegated.

3. Breaking wind requires tolerance, but no more than the ravages of fourteen childbirths.

4. While it's true that your mother-in-law was a happier woman than you, she was also widowed at a young age.

Latina feminism faces unique challenges, like trying to attend feminist committee meetings when you're being driven by your teenaged son, while two preteens are fighting in the car and a snotty-nosed five-year-old with an acid reflux condition vomits on your carpooling committee chairwoman. You finally arrive and the lecture begins, but the teething baby you're breast-feeding is using your nipple as a chew toy and you catch your chauffeur try-ing to download pornography onto his cell phone. You'll have to leave early, because it's past the baby's bedtime and both sets of grandparents are back at the house worrying. There's only so much you can do in such a situation.

CHAPTER 4

U.S. Latinos Under Pressure

You might think that Latinos live under a lot of stress before we finally arrive in the United States, and it's true. But what you might not know is that we also live under a lot of stress after we arrive. It's tempting to wipe your brow and think, "We made it. We have migrated," but that new status is just the beginning of a whole lot of new things to worry about.

Myth #1: Immigrating to the United States will be the happiest day of your life.

The Latino who leaves his country stirs up a lot of mixed feelings and sensations in himself and those around him. He causes sadness and pain to his family, who are going to miss him, the envy of those who wish they were leaving for America but don't have what it takes to do it, and the happiness of his enemies and adversaries, who are glad to see him leave. Everybody waves goodbye and cries, but what lies beneath the surface is a cold war, a competition between him and his friends, family, and fellow citizens who decided to remain in their country. There's a lot at stake. He has to prove to everyone that this American adventure will turn out to be the best decision of his whole life. The expectations are big—to be able to eat, for instance. That leads to our second myth.

Myth #2: Coming to the United States is always a step up.
No matter how bad you are doing in one place, you can always do worse in another. Once the immigrant is here, he realizes that success is not easy. He is willing to work hard, but that's not enough. He also has to be lucky. No matter what, he can't disappoint his loved ones. He has to prove that he made the right choice, and that he's not a loser. Based on a survey I've conducted personally, 69 percent of interviewed Latinos lie about their progress and life quality in the United States when speaking with friends and family back in our home countries. The most common excuse for that kind of behavior is: "I don't want them worrying about me." The truth is many of us are ashamed of what our loved ones—and even worse, our enemies—could think about our lack of achievements in a place everyone calls the land of opportunity.

From all the interviews I've done on this subject, I've selected some of the best lies that U.S. Latinos tell our families back home to hide our real economic status. The usual technique is to tell a lie that has 20 percent truth. Later on, if the fraud surfaces, we could always blame it on a misinterpretation, a misunderstanding, or a "wardrobe malfunction."

- *"The apartment is cozy, and it has a wonderful view"* really means "Twenty of us sleep on the floor of a studio, but we have a poster of Shakira on the wall." We never send photos of where we live, and we don't even give the address to our families (a search on Google Earth could end the charade).

- *"I have the best job I could have ever dreamed about"* really means "I have a job." This isn't even really a lie, because chances are we were unemployed back in our home countries, and having a job—any job—really *was* what we dreamed about.
- *"The kids help a lot at home"* really means "My juvenile delinquent children are playing hooky." The solution here is simple enough: just take your kids to work. When they witness what immigrant parents typically have to do for a living, they won't be able to get back to class fast enough.
- *"Our family is more connected than ever"* really means "We are too scared of Immigration to leave the house."
- *"The house is small, but the heart is big"* really means "I have fourteen illegal immigrants living in my garage, and I can't kick them out because they're all cousins."
- *"My boss has taken a special interest in my work"* really means "He doesn't let me out of his sight for a minute, fearing I'd steal something."
- *"Although we are far away, we'll not lose our roots"* really means "We tried learning English, but it's harder than we thought."
- *"As soon as we make some money, we'll come see you"* really means "If we ever win the lotto, we'll rub it in all of your faces."

Every Latino immigrant must eventually face the hardest exam of his life. Some attempt it after a couple of years, others take ten or more to muster the courage, while others seem intent on putting it off indefinitely. He must face a panel of hard-nosed judges and try his best to impress them. He'll put his best foot forward, but the cross-examination will be brutal. I'm not talking about the citizenship exam. I'm talking about going back to his native country for a visit. No matter how many presents he brings or how handsome he looks stepping off the plane, the returning immigrant will always slip up at some point. He'll take the bait on an apparently innocent question from one of his relatives, which will quickly become a detailed audit of his true feelings and his finances. Yes, you could afford the plane ticket and the nice clothes you arrived in, but did you do it with credit cards? And you can't even afford the minimum monthly payments and so are considering bankruptcy? You left the country fourteen years ago to pursue your dream of a better life, and you are still a restaurant cook? Not that there's anything wrong with a blue-collar job, but I thought it was the land of opportunity. You went to the United States for *that?*

At this point, you could ask: Why would an immigrant—who barely speaks the language, who's discriminated against and socially harassed, who doesn't have many real chances to succeed, and who's scorned in his own country for leaving—decide to stay in the United States, in spite of everything? It's a complex mystery that will require much study. On an unrelated note, did you know that in this country you can lease a new Corvette for $629 a month?

CHAPTER 5

The Latino Family Unit

I should start by saying the root for the English word "family" is the Latin "familia" and it means "household." It referred originally to all the people living under the same roof, whether related by blood or not. Not until the seventeenth and eighteenth century did "family" have the meaning we give the word today.

Truth #1: For Latinos, the meaning of family still is the same as in the middle ages: Every soul living under the same roof is part of the family, though some of them have arrived this morning and nobody knows their names yet. The thing is, among Latinos, when you marry your wife, you are actually marrying her whole family, and you better get along, because you are going to share every piece of your life with them.

To a typical Anglo family, the fact that sons and daughters leave their parents' house to go to college just makes sense, it's a sort of rule of thumb. Your kids are supposed to follow their dreams, which most of the time involves going to a city, working there, finding their soul mate, getting married, and finally having kids of their own. Grandparents and aunts and cousins are seen on Thanksgiving and Christmas, maybe every other year for each side of the family. Grandparents complain about their sons and daughters not visiting them enough, and sons and daughters complain about their mothers phoning them too much. Latinos watch these kinds of stories on TV and are completely mystified by them.

An old Italian saying summarizes the number-one rule of Latino family: "There's nothing better than the family gathered together." This is nothing if not a free pass for four generations to expect shelter under your roof, not to mention close friends, distant cousins, and "aunts" and "uncles" who don't actually appear on the family tree. This motley assembly claims all the same rights and duties of the head of household's firstborn son.

At first sight, this kind of arrangement, with all its discordance between ages, sexes, tastes, schedules, morals, habits, and sometimes even languages, seems to be a kind of hell. Indeed, that's because it is. This is what I've been trying to tell you since the beginning of the chapter.

In the 1970s, Arnold Toynbee, a historian of the world's old civilizations, wrote, "Mankind is surely going to destroy itself unless it succeeds in growing together into something like a single-family." To experience that silly theory in practice himself, Mr. Toynbee should have spent a weekend living with a Latino family. After waiting forty-five minutes to use a toilet, only to find it had been clogged with a rubber ducky, and then to be told he needed to leave so that four girls could tease their hair while a teen boy sneaked a cigarette, and an uncle can't find his pistol— have you seen it?—and how can you think of luxuries like using the bathroom when you didn't go to church today, will there be nice scented seashell soaps for you in hell? That experience would have sufficed for him to edit his theory down to: "Mankind is surely going to destroy itself."

Truth #2: Any excuse is good enough to gather all the family members together.

Birthdays, holidays, baptisms, religious celebrations, graduations, weddings, divorces, burial services, heart surgeries, paydays, Powerball, barbecues, *La Fea Más Bella*, and dominoes are all good reasons to put everything else on hold and spend some time with the family. A strong family unit conveys to its children the meaning of honor, good manners, and respect for the authorities, except for Border Patrol. In my country, Chile, our coat of arms reads "*Por la razon o por la fuerza*" (By reason or by force). That's just a nice family value for the children, no?

Truth #3: Latino families have a profound respect for our elders. This is a value all Latino kids learn as soon as we can walk, when our older brother kicks our legs out from under us. Latinos might work in retirement homes, but we never live in them. Elders are to be catered to, indulged, consulted, and obeyed. This is why we never leave the household and you have forty people living under the same roof . . . nobody wants to miss out on his turn to be an elder!

While a family is a unit that can be studied as a whole, it is also obviously made up of individuals who bring different things to the table. Let's look at some of the more common archetypes.

- *The father.* The boss, the head of the household, the leader, or—as he's secretly called in the poorest families—the one to blame. He wakes up at four a.m. sharp to go to work, having a three-hour bus ride, because he has no car. He comes back home after dusk, so tired he's only able to grab a bite and walk the few steps to his bed. Looking at how tired he is, you can't imagine how he manages to have so many children.

When it comes to the family table, the father takes a seat at its head. He's in charge of the prayers before the first bite, so when he closes his eyes, the rest of the family steals food from his plate, because he always gets the bigger portion. He's also in charge of scaring the hell out of his teenage daughter's boyfriends and teaching his seven-year-old how to burp, when his mother isn't watching.

He immigrated to the United States at age twelve. Anglos see him as a Latino. Latinos in his home country see him as a gringo. He was raised with the belief that hard work is the key to a successful family, though no one told him it would be his hard work and someone else's successful family.

- *The mother.* She takes care of the little ones, does the cleaning, the washing, and the cooking for everybody. She keeps track of the bills and the money and looks for freelance jobs to help make ends meet. When she's not working outside the house she loves to watch *novelas* (Latino soap operas), and when she is working outside the house . . . she finds time to watch them, too.

At the house, she's the one who yells, who cries, who laughs out loud, and who slams the door. Sometimes, all at once. No one dares to suggest she may be watching too many *novelas*.

- *Grandpa.* He immigrated forty years ago. He makes a living on his retirement check plus at his son's expense. He has proudly given the next generation the opportunity to pursue a better future. He is constantly comparing the United States to his native country, where everything was always better, even though he hasn't gone back once. "There was no pollution back home like there is in the United States." Of course there wasn't, because when he left there were no cars and no industry.

- *The great-grandparent.* At ninety-four years old,

Cristián de la Fuente

Latinos always travel with our families. Here I am between takes playing with my daughter, who beats me every time we play *fútbol* (for you, soccer).

he's still walking down the street ogling teenaged girls and challenging hoodlums to fight him.

- *The teenage daughter.* Born in this country, she barely speaks Spanish, so she has almost no interaction whatsoever with the older members of the family. She dresses more expensively than her mother can afford and sexier than her father approves of. Every single day she chooses a different member of the family to start an argument with, and at least weekly she reminds everybody in the house that she can't wait to go to college so she never has to see them again. The family knows that's not going to happen anytime soon, since she's fifteen years old and still in the fifth grade.
- *The kid.* There's always at least one kid. Whether the parents are twenty-five years old or seventy-five, they unfailingly have a kid no older than ten. Without exception, the youngest is also the most centered family member. He speaks English and Spanish, he's a hardworking student, and he practices a variety of sports. He doesn't understand why the grown-ups argue so much about everything, but he never gets involved. You might be wondering: How could one of the children be *so different* from the rest of the family? Watch your *novelas* and you will get a hint!

After years of study, the Italian philosopher Pasquale Bertone was finally able to produce a formula that has become the most accurate mathematic representation of any given Latino family:

Latino Family = Father + Mother + Grandpa + Great-grandpa + (Uncle × 3) + (Cousin × 4) + (Kids × 3 / Neighbor) + (Godfathers + Godmothers) + (Friends × 6) + (Recently Arrived Illegal Immigrants × 2)

Pasquale Bertone perfected this formula after three years of living with a Latino family in their house in Santa Monica, California. Today, Mr. Bertone resides in Miami, which is to say, he's an inpatient at one of Miami's finest psychiatric institutions.

CHAPTER 6

Every Woman Wants to Be Latina

When I was on *Dancing with the Stars*, my partner Cheryl Burke—who's a Filipina—invited me to the Asian Excellence Awards ceremony, where she won in the category Favorite TV Personality 2008. When I was hanging out there before the ceremony, most of the people were speaking in Asian languages. It was understandable; it was an Asian night full of Asian personalities.

A couple of months later I was invited to the American Latino Media Arts Awards, or ALMA Awards, which are distinctions awarded to Latino performers who promote positive portrayals of Latinos in the entertainment field. I was nothing short of astonished when I arrived there to find . . . Cheryl Burke hanging out among our Latina peers. Wasn't she Asian? I know what you are thinking: I'm Latino and I attended the Asian awards . . . but I was presenting a category.

When I was coming back home after the show, I couldn't keep out of my mind the fact that the venue was full of women who weren't Latinas. That's when I realized that even if they don't accept it, at some point every woman wants to be Latina.

The Latina is a female paradigm that takes our breath away, and I don't mean that she hits us in the stomach because she didn't like the way we ogled her—which in fact happens all the time—but instead because of her exuberance. She has been portrayed a thousand times in movies as the ravenous and outgoing femme fatale with a voluptuous body, colorful style of dress, and always more than ready for physical love. But let me tell you, not everything you see in movies is true . . . sometimes they wear black. Let's look at the five biggest myths about Latinas.

Myth #1: The Latina always looks happy.
I think this one is true. When I come home, my wife is always smiling—unless I come back at three in the morning. In that case, she is baring her fangs, but it still looks like a smile!

Myth #2: Latinas have "curves."
This is also true. Just look what Jennifer Lopez was able to do in your country with a figure that in our culture is considered average.

Myth #3: Latinas are more willing to engage in the love game.
It remains a myth. On the one hand, they are, like all Latin people, at the mercy of their crazy, hot-blooded passion. On the other, you have to meet them halfway: If you are old, bald, short, illiterate, and poor . . . not even the "Latin heat" is going to help your sorry case.

Myth #4: Latinas can kill for their men.
Half-truth. They only use their men as an excuse for what they were going to do anyway.

Myth # 5: Latinas are more emotional than your average female. Undeniable truth. How do I know? If every man has scars, Latino husbands' backs look like Rambo's.

These five myths have created a kind of *Latina Mystique.* Non-Latina women are attracted to Latina behavior, and they often try to copycat them, thinking it will add some spice to their lives. Would this work? I don't know, but let's find out.

It's time to help my Anglo female readers. You need a study that would lead you to understand Latinas, their behavior, their mysterious way of thinking. Let's do an imaginary social experiment for a minute. What would happen if two groups of women, Latinas and Anglos, were challenged to live together under the same roof, without men, for thirty days?

Note: This is a good idea for a reality show, so if you are a TV producer, please don't steal it from me!

Day 1: Both groups of women arrive at the house they're going to live in. The Latinas demand the first shift to shower, and they take three hours and fifteen minutes—each. The house runs out of hot water, and the Latinas drown out the complaints of the Anglos by blow-drying their hair.

Day 5: The Anglo women are not ashamed of their bodies by any means, so they walk through the house buck-naked. The Latinas beat the hell out of one of them for having too nice a body, which is "conceited." The injured girl quits.

Day 10: By now, the Latinas have used up all their own makeup, then the Anglos' makeup, and are trying to make eye shadow by mixing flour and guacamole.

Day 14: In a nice gesture toward coexistence, the Latinas offer to fix a meal for both groups to share. The Anglos, pleased, accept. Five gallons of lard somehow make it into three courses.

Day 15: 911 is called when the Anglos are diagnosed with acute cholesterol poisoning.

Day 21: The Anglos ask permission to go shopping. As they wait for an answer, the Latinas have already made backless halter tops out of the living room drapes and kitchen tablecloth.

Day 28: The bathroom drain clogs due to the amount of hair the Latinas lose when they brush. A male plumber arrives to clean the drain. Five minutes later, the Latinas have him locked in their room and are demanding at least four more handsome plumbers before the end of the day or they'll kill an Anglo girl.

Day 30: End of the experiment. As soon as the door is opened, the Anglos flee the house like bats out of hell. The Latinas phone their families, and within twenty minutes, 145 relatives have moved in. It will either take thirty police officers to remove them or one INS officer for them to remove themselves.

To sum it all up, this exercise gives us a great understanding of many Latina virtues. They take hygiene very seriously. They have curves, but they also have modesty and expect it in other women, especially those with nicer bodies. They can be very inventive and thrifty. They are able cooks and can eat insane amounts of cholesterol without becoming poisoned. They are not afraid to take the first step in the love game. And they love their families.

If you are a female non-Latina reader, you have a lot to admire and emulate here. If I were you, I'd hold off on the cholesterol virtue and start by taking the first step in the love game. Even if you never become a true Latina, I'm pretty sure you are going to enjoy trying that one out.

CHAPTER 7

AROUND LATIN AMERICA IN 80 DAYS—PRACTICAL LEARNING

One good way to understand where Latinos in the United States are coming from is by knowing, well, where we came from. If you want to learn quickly and accurately, grab your mental passport and get ready for the armchair adventure of a lifetime.

First stop, Mexico. Bordered by four American states—California, Arizona, New Mexico, and Texas—it's the most populous Spanish-speaking country in the world, with around 100 million people. DF is its capital city (acronym that stands for "Federal District" in Spanish). It's one of the most crowded in the world—15 million inhabitants—and their biggest problem is air pollution, closely followed by poverty, crime, and drinking water that will kill an Anglo dead. As soon as you put one foot into the airport, cabdrivers will intuit that you are an American tourist and approach you, asking, "Taxi? Hotel?" Luckily for everyone, those two words are written and pronounced identically in both languages.

You'll answer, "Yes," which is the only answer they understand.

Even though your hotel is seven blocks from the airport, the taxi fare is going to be one hundred dollars. Call it an "Anglo discount."

Once checked in, there's nothing better than taking a walk to have a glimpse of the locals. You stroll a couple of blocks, and suddenly you have a very familiar feeling: Doesn't it seem like you're in Los Angeles? There are Mexicans everywhere. The difference is when you first bite that taco you bought on the street. In Mexico, spicy means *really* spicy. There's no time to "think outside the bun" here. You have to "think inside the *baño*."

You keep walking, but ten minutes later, the combination of *tripitas* and carbon monoxide makes you start to feel a little dizzy. When you open your eyes, you're in the Hospital Juárez. Latin American treatment, American-sized medical bill.

You resume your trip heading south. Next destination: Colombia, South America's northernmost country. There are about 40 million people. Bogotá is its capital city, 2,366 miles south of Washington, D.C. Here you have to deal with street merchants, estimated at a whopping 20 percent of all commerce workers in the city. They seize upon every piece of public space selling everything you could think of, legal or not.

As soon as you put one foot down in El Dorado International Airport of Bogotá, cabdrivers will approach you, intuiting that you're an American tourist. They'll try to speak English: "Taxi? Hotel? DEA headquarters?"

Strange as it may seem, and regardless of how far from the airport your hotel is, the taxi fare will be the same as Mexico's, one hundred dollars.

Once checked in, and with your luggage safe in the hotel vault, there's nothing better than to take a walk and have a glimpse of the local people. Some friends of yours who often talk nonsense might have tipped you off about the Colombian streets: "Beware of the drug dealers." This is nothing but a slander. Believe me, when you're walking down the streets of any Latin American country, the least you have to worry about is drug dealers. Prostitution, kidnappings, and murders will keep you plenty busy.

As you wait to cross the street, a little kid asks you for a peso Colombiano, the official currency. You look at him, touched, and give him a dollar bill. The boy quickly calls his friends, and thirty seconds later, they're all staring at the bill, their eyes popping out of their heads. Just as you smile at their childlike enthusiasm, they suddenly lunge at you, going simultaneously for your wallet and your eyes. Where has the innocence gone? I don't know, but I wouldn't look for it on the streets of Bogotá, Colombia.

When you wake up, you're in the Hospital Santa Clara. Latin American treatment, drug lord–sized medical bill.

Once you're back on your feet, you decide to get to the bottom of your subject, and one of the two southernmost South American countries is my beloved Chile. Chile's population is estimated at around 16 million people. The capital city is Santiago, where I was born, located 5,021 miles south of Washington, D.C. Currently, Chile is one of South America's most stable and prosperous nations, which is like being the tallest midget or the smartest mule.

As soon as you put one foot down in the Comodoro Arturo Merino Benitez International Airport in Santiago, the cabdrivers, intuiting that you're an American tourist, will start to fight among themselves, punching, kicking, and eye gouging one another in order to secure you as a passenger. The winner will ask you: "Taxi? Hotel?"

This time, the fare will be two hundred dollars, but half of it will go to the cabbie's medical bill, since he dislocated his shoulder fighting for your business. Chile is known worldwide for its wines, so you decide to treat yourself to a good dinner and try to forget all the bad experiences you've had so far.

Once at the restaurant, you enjoy a juicy steak and a cabernet. Then the unexpected happens—a group of four armed, hooded men burst in and make everyone lie down on the floor. They quickly start taking everyone's money, jewelry, and even their clothes. The *carabineros* (Chilean police) show up, and after a quick firefight, the two surviving robbers are taken prisoner. Meanwhile, you have fainted, and when you open your eyes again you're in the Hospital Clínico Universidad Católica de Chile. Latin American treatment, vineyard owner–sized bill.

Back on your feet again, you board a direct flight to the Caribbean, where you'll have the chance to visit three islands full of potential U.S. immigrants: Puerto Rico, Dominican Republic, and Cuba. In all of them, the taxi fare will be one hundred dollars. After visiting six countries, you come to understand that a hundred dollars is the Latin American airport taxi's flat rate for Anglos.

You take your first walk in Puerto Rico, and you see people whose faces resemble others you've seen in New York. You take your first walk in the Dominican Republic, and you also see people whose faces resemble others you've seen in New York. You take your first walk in Cuba, and people approach you, saying: "Would you please take me with you to New York?"

In Puerto Rico, you'll be invited to dance salsa, and if you're lucky enough, a lady will ask you to escort her to your hotel room. In the Dominican Republic, you'll be invited to dance *bachata*, and if you're lucky enough, a lady will ask you to escort her to your hotel room. In Cuba, you'll be invited to dance mambo, and even if you're not lucky at all, a lady will ask you to escort her to the United States.

You've spent twelve hard, grueling, yet fascinating weeks on the road. You've mastered the art of everyday life in Latin American countries. You have seen and lived for yourself the experiences that make up the backgrounds of your new neighbors. You've embraced different communities and learned valuable lessons about the heterogeneous group we call Latinos. Now you long for home, and you are more than ready to go back to the United States. On your flight back, you realize how fortunate you are to have been born in this country, where at least the rules seem reasonable and clear.

Your plane lands, and you are home. You walk quickly and excitedly toward the passport booth, where an officer checks the stamps of the countries you've visited on your trip. He kindly asks you to follow him to a small interrogation room, in which you will be treated to a cavity search because you've been in Colombia. You will be grilled about your communist affiliations, because you've been in Cuba. They demand to know how many illegal immigrants you helped to cross the border in Mexico, and they take your fingerprints as a "person of interest" related to the robbery you witnessed in Chile. Four and a half hours later, you're released.

In the taxi heading home, you smile with relief as soon as you start recognizing the streets of your neighborhood. Despite having enjoyed the trip, things are definitely more comfortable at home. Finally, the taxi stops at the curb in front of your house and the driver says: "That'll be a hundred bucks."

CHAPTER 8

Differences Between Anglos and Latinos, Part i

Archimedes once said of the lever, "Give me a place on which to stand, and I will move the earth." Like Archimedes, we will also need to employ two fixed points, the Latino and Anglo worlds, if we are to leverage a better understanding between them. The task I'm going to pursue next involves trying to explain how Latinos and Anglos react differently when we face the same extreme situations. My father used to say that anything you need to know about a person can be observed at the dinner table and on the playing field. I'll try to apply the same principle here, but pushed to its logical limit. If we can define the limits and boundaries of Latino behavior versus Anglo behavior in life's most radical scenarios, hopefully we will have a better picture of how both can be moved to sympathy.

- *Situation A.* The National Hurricane Center issues a hurricane warning. A Category 5 storm is on its way to your city. The government declares a mandatory evacuation within twenty-four hours.

- **Anglo family:** Spends two hours packing their most treasured family possessions and evacuates.
- **Latino family:** Spends two hours eating everything in the fridge, then lines up outside the bathroom to evacuate.
- **Anglo family:** They put the shutters up to cover the windows.
- **Latino family:** Windows were bricked up when we moved in.
- **Anglo family:** They withdraw some cash from the ATM and head to the shelter.
- **Latino family:** Head straight to the shelter and bust out our Latino ATM cards—the tortillas we will sell to the other evacuees.

- *Situation B.* The family's seven-year-old son gets an F on his report card. What does the father do?
  - **Anglo father:** Grounds the kid.
  - **Latino father:** Threatens to put the kid in the ground.
  - **Anglo father:** Tells a tutor they'd better start home lessons immediately.
  - **Latino father:** Tells the teacher he'd better start running immediately.
  - **Anglo father:** Finally comes to an understanding— kids are just kids, and they talk about it as a family.
  - **Latino father:** Finally comes to an understanding—an F means the kid is attending school.

- *Situation C.* A policeman catches you driving under the influence.

- **Female Anglo:** Tries to conceal that she had a cosmo.
- **Latina:** Tries to reveal that she has cleavage.
- **Female Anglo:** Hands officer registration.
- **Latina:** Registers officer's hands.
- **Female Anglo:** Smiles, because she has learned her lesson.
- **Latina:** Smiles, because she is on *COPS!*

- *Situation D.* You receive a call from your sister. Grandma passed away a few minutes ago from natural causes. She was ninety-seven.
  - **Anglo grandchild:** Wishes she could attend the funeral services, but she booked tickets to Cancun Spring Break two months in advance.
  - **Latino grandchild:** Tells her sister that she knows all of this already, since the three of them have had to share a bed for the past two years.
  - **Anglo grandchild:** Starts thinking, "Am I going to inherit her diamonds?"
  - **Latino grandchild:** Starts thinking, "Am I going to inherit her diabetes?"
  - **Anglo grandchild:** Stays awake all night recalling fond memories.
  - **Latino grandchild:** Stays awake all night on a recalled mattress.

- *Situation E.* Your teenaged daughter says she's five months pregnant.
  - **Anglo mother:** May I know who the father is?
  - **Latino mother:** Do *you* know who the father is?
  - **Anglo mother:** I'm going to call the family therapist.
  - **Latino mother:** I'm going to call the statutory rapist.
  - **Anglo mother:** We're going to send you away to

have this baby. When you come back, we'll say it's mine.

- **Latino mother:** You will spend the rest of your pregnancy in your room. When the kid is born, we'll say it's mine.

CHAPTER 9

So Your Daughter Is Marrying a Latino . . .

You may think it won't happen to you, but if you have a daughter between thirteen and seventy-five years old, this chapter is relevant to you. Cupid could draw back his bow and let fly a *churro* right into your daughter's heart. But it's not all bad. Like anything else, there are pros and cons.

PROS OF YOUR DAUGHTER MARRYING A LATINO:

- Free Spanish classes for your grandchildren.
- Free valet parking while you sleep, with two hundred bonus miles on your odometer.
- You will see your daughter more often, because she and her new husband will move in.
- Your daughter might learn how to cook from her husband's mother.
- People outside the Home Depot looking for work will greet you by name and offer you discounts.

- He won't insist your daughter be "just a house-wife"; she'll also have to be the primary bread-winner.
- You will save on health care, since you will treat everything with home remedies recommended by a *bruja* named Estrella.
- The whole family can learn how to dance, unless he is from Chile.

CONS OF YOUR DAUGHTER MARRYING A LATINO:

- Chino, Triste, Frisky, Lil' Frog, and Loco . . . literally *cons*.
- Once your wife meets your "macho Latino/Latin lover" son-in-law, she is going to expect more from you.
- Your house will always be full of friends . . . Chino, Triste, Frisky, Lil' Frog, and Loco.
- Your grandchildren will call you "gringo."
- Your phone bill will have a lot of unclaimed calls to South America.
- You will need to travel to meet the boy's parents, and it could be a one-way trip.

TOP TEN THINGS NON-LATINO PARENTS SHOULD KNOW ABOUT LATINOS:

- We get our wives pregnant frequently. Occasion-ally, we get other men's wives pregnant, too.
- We like sports. We love to win. We hate to lose. We are not good sports about it.
- We like to hug in-laws. And sometimes grab

their asses if they're hot. Don't freak out, it's cultural.

- When we win a bet, we want the money right away. When we lose, please understand we are paying for our grandma's medication and grandpa's citizenship application.
- We expect you to pay for the wedding. And the honeymoon. And the car. And the house.
- We don't like to pay taxes. Nobody does, but we actually don't pay them.
- We might have kids from previous relationships. Don't be alarmed if some of them knock on your door asking for a loan. Go ahead and give it to them. Better yet, give it to us and we'll pass it along.
- We don't really have a work-from-home job, we just say that so we can hang out in the beautiful house you bought us.
- We love your daughter more than anything in the world, and we will protect her with our life . . . especially from the mailman or Starbucks barista she innocently says hello to.

I have to make a clarification. Not being happy with your daughter's love choice doesn't necessarily mean you discriminate against people. In other words, you could be president of a nonprofit organization whose main goal is to help immigrants, but let's say your daughter is dating Pedro, a Latino boy with two missing teeth who works the night shift as a clerk in a gas station near your home. Pedro has to go, and it's not because you are prejudiced against Latinos. You have to come up with a plan to destroy their relationship, and you will be required to be almost unreal with the kind of statements you make about him. These are a few claims you should choose from; feel free to pick the one that best fits the occasion.

- I have a confession to make: I'm gay. Not only that, I'm in love with Pedro, your boyfriend, and he loves me back. He said he's dating you to stay close to me.
- What happened to my fingers? It's nothing. Some of Pedro's most delightful friends stopped by to ask him to repay some money. He wasn't home, and they didn't believe me.
- I've run a background check on Pedro and I've found out he's not single. He became widowed four times in the last couple of years, and all of his wives died from poison.
- Pedro is taking a phone call in my room. I heard something about a shipment from Colombia under *your* name.
- Pedro took your mother to the house of a Latino healer who can make her headaches go away. It was something involving animal sacrifices, I didn't pay attention.
- There's a thirteen-year-old girl at the front door who wants to tell you a secret concerning Pedro. No, she's not claiming to be his daughter; she says she's his wife.

If none of this works, perhaps the "Don Juan" myth of the Latin lover is more than a legend. Why in the world does your daughter like Pedro, anyway? You think about it and recall your affair thirty years ago with your parents' housekeeper, Lupita. Since your daughter has your genes, the conclusion is obvious: Parents are always to blame for their children's problems, so if you're going to ground them, you should go ahead and ground yourself, too.

CHAPTER 10

What *Not* to Call a Latino . . .

Latinos in the United States are subjected to a wide variety of upsetting labels. I'm talking about ethnic slurs. The questions are: Where do they come from? When and why are they used? And why am I asking you questions as though you could answer me?

The labels we're about to discuss are usually forbidden among Latinos. We would certainly be insulted to hear them, but as John Leguizamo once said: "The use of a forbidden word over and over again is a way to drain it of its negative force. The point is that the word's suppression gives it the viciousness. If you repeat the word as many times as you can, it'll lose its meaning." Okay, that is interesting food for thought, but let me give you some advice. If you are white, he's not talking to you. If you are going to "repeat the word as many times as you can," make sure you are alone in your panic room or nuclear bunker.

Spic. Supposedly this word derives from the mispronunciation of the word "speak" by Hispanic Americans (No spic el ingles!). I think the Anglos adopted it to get even with us ever since we started using the slang term "gringos" on them. According to one popular version of the etymology, the term gringo comes from "green go home!" which was sometimes the reaction of Mexicans when U.S. soldiers passed by, referring to the color of the uniforms. Isn't it strange how every time Latinos mispronounce something, it becomes a new slang word, but every time Anglos mispronounce something, it becomes the official name of a state?

Chicano. Another mispronunciation, this term derives from the pre-Columbian word the Indians in Mexico used to describe themselves: "Meshicas," which later became "Meshicanos" or even "Shicanos." These days it refers to American citizens of Mexican descent who identify as non-Anglo, being "neither from here, nor from there." While a few Latinos consider the word an ethnic slur, it's considered a politically loaded rather than a derogatory term. If you are a Chicano reading this book, you might not agree, but I think most of the 40 million Latinos in this country feel "neither from here, nor from there." I've been in this country for just ten years, and look at me: I speak "Spanglish," I eat *aguacate* with French fries, and I play football with my hands. It's just a matter of time before we are all Chicanos.

Anchor baby. No, this is not the hot new collectible doll that stores can't keep in stock and you are forced to buy off eBay for $200 so that your niece does not die from disappointment. But now that you mention it, I could have made a fortune on that idea. So, anchor babies—under the provisions of the Immigration and Nationality Act of 1965, a child born of an immigrant in the United States is allowed to choose American citizenship automatically. Therefore, this very young immigrant could sponsor citizenship for family members who are still abroad. It sounds like a great scheme for getting citizenship for your whole village, except for one catch. An anchor baby will have to wait until his eighteenth birthday to start the sponsorship. Immigrants who are willing to leave our countries want the American dream now, not eighteen years from now. We will have missed all of our winning Quick Picks by then. Believe me, if all you had to do to get citizenship for yourself in this country was to have a child here, you'd see Latinos having sex on every corner of every city in the United States. I know that's literally happening, but it's not for citizenship.

Beaner. This one usually refers to people of Mexican descent, since they traditionally have a lot of frijoles (beans) in their cooking. Nowadays, almost none of my Mexican friends find this term particularly offensive. They laugh about it the first time you use the term, they smile politely the second time, and the third time, they shoot your dog. To me, food-related slurs are the silliest of all, because they aren't really negative. You have to be very stupid to be offended by a name based on what you eat. "Oh, yes? Are you calling us beaners?" Well, you Anglos are ... baconers! Big deal.

Nuyorican. Although this is not an ethnic slur, I include it because it can be used as a demeaning term to imply a Latino is overly assimilated into U.S. culture. It comes from a mixture of the words "New York" and "Puerto Rican." Personally, I like this one, because it has a kind of pleasant musicality to the ear. As someone from Chile living in Los Angeles, what can I call myself? "Chilosangelean"? That's just a mess.

Wetback. This is one of the more derogatory terms, referring to illegal immigrants swimming across the Rio Grande. I don't get it personally, because if I had to cross a river as fast as I could, I don't think I'd choose the backstroke. Instead, Border Patrol would mistake me for an Olympian training to break the 2000m butterfly world record. I'd swim so fast that instead of getting shot at or chased by dogs, I'd get an endorsement deal with Speedo and a cameo on *Entourage*.

Marielito. This is the term used to describe the more than 100,000 Cubans who fled to the United States from the port of Mariel in 1980 after Castro said something like: "Anyone who wants to leave is free to go." When U.S. officials found out that a number of the exiles had been released from Cuban jails and mental health facilities, the exodus was ended by mutual agreement between the two countries. The refugees would be allowed to stay, but the whole episode wound up creating a perception of "Marielitos" as criminals. Today, this derogatory term is meaningless, since pretty much all Latinos are perceived as criminals. Believe me, I'm reading scripts for five different roles, and they all end up shanked in a prison yard within the first five minutes of the movie.

Balsero. This term refers to Latinos arriving by sea using a *balsa* (raft). It's used mostly in Miami to describe the illegal immigrants from Cuba, because the island is only ninety miles away from this country. Basically, a "Balsero" is a "Marielito" without the mutual consent of both governments . . . or a boat. They make their own rafts and hope they can float to freedom. Believe me, if Cubans could learn how to build a bicycle plane, there would be a cloud of them over Miami International Airport every single day.

Fresh Off the Boat. This term was first used to described people of Asian origin, but now it means any immigrants who have not yet learned this country's culture, language, and customs. But hey, what do you expect? It's not so easy. I'd like to see a group of Anglos fly to, say, Japan and try to assimilate into their culture.

But wait, I actually saw that—it was a reality show on TV last season! Latinos immigrate, work hard for low pay, and are disrespected and denied opportunities at every turn. Anglos do exactly the same thing, but they manage to get sponsors, lucrative syndication contracts, and fame as reality television stars. Take a bow, America, you win the game show of life!

CHAPTER 11

So You're Dating the Little Sister of a Latino . . .

It's Saturday night in the coolest bar in the city. You can only be admitted by showing an invitation hand-signed by the owner, and even that might not be enough. It's that exclusive. The enormous bouncers greet you with a fist bump. The mood inside is ideal, the music is mellow, the women are hot, and, of course, all of them are looking at you. Have you ever been in a situation like that? Of course you have, you're a citizen of the United States. You feel like that almost every day.

You have come to the bar by yourself, to celebrate what was for you a great day, one of those days everything goes just right—you like what you see in the mirror, and you feel powerful and on top of the world. Have you ever felt like that? Of course you have, you're a citizen of the United States. You feel like that almost every day.

You ask for a drink, something smooth. After four more smooth drinks, you feel pretty smooth yourself—perhaps enough to approach *her*: on top of a speaker, dancing like crazy, shaking her hips and flipping her hair like in a shampoo commercial. She seems different, maybe deaf. Blond, tall, good curves, beautiful eyes—you guess these things, because you can't take your eyes off of her chest.

Two minutes later, you're both in the V.I.P. lounge. An hour later, after a lot of laughter and more drinks, you learn her name is Taylor, and she says she's going to the ladies' room to retouch her makeup. There's no need, she's stunning. The last thing you remember is Taylor's lower back sensually swaying while she walks away. Blackout.

Next thing you know, it is morning and the sunlight comes pouring in through the window. You're in bed, naked, you have a hell of a headache and everything is spinning. There's an issue: It's not your bed. It's not even your house. Questions keep popping into your mind, as you swear to God you will never drink alcohol again in your life. What happened last night? Whose house is this? Who killed JFK? You look around the room for clues as to whose house this could be. There's no need to rummage; over the nightstand there's a picture of . . . Taylor. Yes! Yes! Oh, my god! Yeah, baby! Victory! You scored with the hottest girl!

You wonder where your new beauty is, perhaps fixing you breakfast? You walk across the room naked, excited, delighted, and slightly shocked. You don't have a clue about what happened last night, but if you woke up here, well, can't you assume the whole nine yards?

As you're about to call out the name of your beloved, something hanging on the wall catches your eye. It's a high school diploma, dated just two years ago, issued to: Guadalupe Taylor Gonzalez. It seems "Taylor" is Latina. Okay, so maybe your dreams of a typical all-American family need some adjustment, but it's still not a bad deal. It's not like you're a racist, and Taylor—err, Guadalupe—is one of the most attractive girls you've ever seen.

The only people who would disagree are her bratty brothers and sisters, sixteen of whom are eating breakfast in the kitchen without even suspecting you're in their house.

You hear some voices coming from the other side of the house—which is the next room. The conversation quickly becomes an argument, and you can clearly hear an angry masculine voice vehemently uttering phrases like: "Gringo?" and "I'll kill him!" That's enough to know it's time to jump out the window.

Two days later, the phone rings. The first thing you hear is Taylor's sweet and tender voice saying, "I love you." That's how Latinas are! One single night together, nobody knows for sure what did or did not happen, and already she's saying "I love you."

You try to convince her that it won't work—there is the difference of age, the difference of cultures, and the difference between being alive and being murdered by her relatives. She won't listen. There is good news: the voice you heard was not her father, but her little brother, Lalo. The bad news is that her "little" brother Lalo is six feet four, 250 pounds, was just released from jail, and handles all the "family business." Having these elements in mind, there are two options to consider:

1. **Use excuses to get rid of her.** You have to be very careful if you're going to go with this one. The last thing you'd want is an angry Latina, or worse, her angry, ex-convict, "business-handling" brother. Here are some examples you could try, at your own risk, of course:
   - "I've been drafted into the army, and I'm leaving this afternoon for the Middle East." If she doesn't buy it, you'd better be prepared to actually go to the Middle East.

- "I want to be ready to meet your family. I'm going to take a three-year Spanish course, in Spain." She'll wait, and so will Lalo, who is excited that you'll understand the Spanish insults he'll call you while he's punching your face.
- "I have a sex change surgery scheduled for tomorrow." The risk here is the possibility her brother is looking for a date, and he'd be interested in seeing how you look after the operation. Sometimes it seems like you're going to end up being part of this family no matter what.

2. **Win over her brother.** If we get to this point, I have to assume that plan one failed. That means she didn't buy your excuses, Lalo is on his way over, and out of respect for your family, Taylor has requested he "make it look like an accident"— thank God that girl loves you. Don't lose hope, you still have these tactics to try:
   - "My father is a congressman. We can get your criminal record cleaned up and fix your credit rating." Bribery has a long and cherished role in Latin American politics, so he'll be touched by your cultural sensitivity.
   - "I'm undercover INS and you are busted!" Hopefully Lalo thinks all Latinos are eligible for deportation, even third-generation Americans like himself.
   - "I'm the casting coordinator for a new soap opera called *Painful Love*, and I believe you'd be great for the main role." No Latino will ever resist this kind of offer. In fact, it was while avenging my own sister that I got my start as an actor in *novelas*.

One last tip: Before rushing into a decision, listen to whatever Taylor has to say. Often we make the mistake of thinking we know everything, and we miss pieces of information that could save our lives. The following examples are things Taylor could say on the phone while her brother is on his way over to "have a talk" with you:

1. I'm pregnant, and we are a very religious family.

2. If you don't marry me, I'll be deported next month.

These change nothing. In fact, they make things worse for you. But then there is the possibility of:

3. That night? No, nothing happened between us. I mean, you had a blackout and I felt sorry for you, so I let you sleep it off at my house.

Number three is a bittersweet moment. Sad, because your dream of having scored with the hottest woman in the bar was an illusion. But it is also happy, provided you can convince Taylor to tell her brother the truth *before* he kicks in your front door and front teeth.

CHAPTER 12

So You Want to Score with a Latina . . .

Yes, I am getting married here. As you may have heard, Latinas usually need a whole police squad to get their boyfriends to sign the marriage license. In my case, it was the Chilean air force aerobatic team.

Cristián de la Fuente

Latina girls are like the Founding Fathers: they think all men have been created equal. Equally lazy, messy, and horny like dogs, and who want to use women for sex and then dump them. We must fight against that myth. And I'm living proof that it's a myth, because I've been happily married for many years, to a Latina, no less. As you can see, my marital status—plus my personal experience before my marriage—gives me the right to be recognized as an expert in the field of scoring with Latinas. Here are some tips that can came in handy:

TOP FIVE THINGS YOU SHOULD DEFINITELY SAY TO A LATINA:

5. I'm learning Spanish. How do I say you are beautiful . . . *Bouhnitah?*

4. Sure, your brother can borrow my convertible anytime he wants.

3. You want to have eleven kids? Me too! We could have our own soccer team!

2. Family is so important, it would be my dream to live with twenty relatives in one house.

1. Yes, it is a Rolex.

What I'm going to do is create hypothetical situations and then advise you on how you can improve your chances in each of them to score with a Latina. You must already know how to woo a woman, so that we can explore how to proceed with a Latino woman. This text is not intended to be redundant with other, basic descriptions and techniques of hitting on girls. We won't start from scratch: how to be nice, sympathetic, make her laugh through a casual chat, buying her flowers and heart-shaped chocolates, becoming emotionally distant, exploiting her vain and competitive nature, and preying on her insecurities—things a man your age ought to know by now. If you don't, go and read *Dating for Dummies* and then come back to this chapter. Once we're on the same page, we can start creating game plans related to the following scenarios, based on Latinas from three different social levels.

Case #1: You and Maria are coworkers with a lot in common, starting with the fact that you both work in the same office. Maria isn't working with you directly so much as she's working on behalf of an industrial cleaning company under contract with your building. This is a key detail since it prompts all kinds of accusations of class exploitation, manager-worker power imbalances, the dominant culture assuming unlimited license, and socioeconomic intimidation equal to coercion. I think these theories are created by evil and lonely people who don't want us to find our soul mates anytime, ever, much less at six fifteen in the broom closet.

You stop leaving the office when you're supposed to. You work later and later, hoping to see her. Finally, you get the nerve to ask her out, she accepts, and today is the big day. What are you going to do tonight? What will you discuss? Office talk is out of the question, and you barely know anything about her. Take note of the following tips and go with them, and you'll score for sure:

- Tip # 1: Take her to a midlevel-priced restaurant: In an expensive one she'd feel out of place, and in a cheap one she'd spend the night greeting friends.

- Tip # 2: Don't pick her up at home; instead meet her at the destination. There's no need to meet her parents, grandparents, cousins, siblings, aunts, and uncles before your first date, to say nothing of her kids.
- Tip # 3: At the end of the evening, take her back to your place and think through the consequences of what you are going to do there. If you try to kiss her, her next son could very well have your name with a "junior" added to the end.

Case #2: You and Lucia are coworkers at a restaurant. She's the cook and you're the maître d'. You shared countless evenings of crepes and customers' complaints, until you fell in love with the unique way she spit on the plates of those who sent back their dishes to the kitchen. Finally, fueled by determination, you got the nerve to ask her out, she accepted, and today is the big day. What are you going to do tonight?

- Tip # 1: Take her to a midlevel-priced restaurant: In an expensive one she'd leave you sitting by yourself while she applies for a job, and in a cheap one she'd recognize her mother's cooking.
- Tip # 2: Don't pick her up at home. You don't want her kids to start calling you "Daddy" before your first date.
- Tip # 3: At the end of the evening, take her back to her place, look her straight in the eye, and ask her if she dreams of getting married: If she an-

swers "yes," kiss her immediately. If she answers "no," take off as fast as you can, because the man about to step out of her house aiming a gun is her husband.

Case #3: You and Elena have known each other for a while. She's the Harvard-educated owner of your firm, and you're one of the many lawyers who work for her. She's been divorced four times, and she's only twenty-five—and that's why she owns the firm. Many Latino women use their divorces as a way to go up the wealth ladder. But you don't care about that. You are sure it'll be different with you. Deep in your heart, you know you are Elena's soul mate.

Finally, fueled by determination, you got the nerve to ask her out, she accepted, and today is the big day. What are you going to do tonight?

- Tip # 1: Take her to whatever kind of restaurant, regardless of the price level, but keep in mind you must let *her* pick up the bill. That's going to make her feel you respect her.
- Tip # 2: Don't pick her up at home; on the contrary, ask her to pick you up. Letting her drive is going to make her feel you respect her.
- Tip # 3: At the end of the evening, ask her to take you back home and say good night without even trying to kiss her. If you played your cards right, she will be so bored of this routine that she'll demand to be taken to your bedroom and disrespected.

CHAPTER 13

So Your Wife Is Latina and You Want a Divorce . . .

I want to begin by thanking God that I'm sharing ideas rather than personal experiences within this chapter. I hope with all of my heart that you're reading this chapter for entertainment value, and you're not really in the situation the title describes. If you are, you haven't made one mistake but two: First, having married a Latina, and second, thinking you can get rid of her.

A Latina will go much further than the average woman, who after her divorce is satisfied by merely taking away her ex-husband's home, job, children, social standing, and money. A Latina will want more. She wants to tear his guts apart, drink his blood, and donate all of his organs to science—while he's still alive. She won't care, because to her, he is dead, even if his pitiful screams suggest otherwise. Are you scared? Watch out, close the book! She's behind you right now! Ha ha, just kidding. Got you!

For our purposes, we're assuming you want a divorce and she doesn't. Any other scenario is not a problem, since whether she asks for it or it's a mutual decision, it will all come down to money and custody—and her getting all of both. Unfortunately, that's not our case. Our case involves pride, and worse, a woman's pride, and truly catastrophic: a Latina's pride. Lupita still loves you. Lupita cannot comprehend why you've made this decision. Let's start answering the four key questions.

1. Why . . . did you marry Lupita in the first place?

Obviously, because you were in love. You fell in love with her looks, her scent, and the sexiness of a woman who naturally swayed her hips as she walked, with a nice rack and a pair of beautiful, thin legs. Today, ten years and a hundred pounds later, that love has left town, and in its suitcase is her scent, sexiness, and sense of humor. She used to get out of bed at midnight, wearing one of your shirts, just to fix you a sandwich. These days at midnight, you find yourself washing your shirts while she's eating a sandwich in bed. You promised to love and protect your wife until death did you part, but the woman to whom you made that promise was apparently eaten by the troll dropping crumbs on your pillow.

2. What . . . did you do to marry her?

You convinced Lupita's father, Don Manuel, that you were a good man who was going to respect her and treat her well. We'll never know whether he blessed the union because of that or the fact that by marrying Lupita, you made her a legal resident.

3. When . . . did you first notice your marriage wasn't working out?

Two years ago, on Valentine's Day, you came home with two expensive seats for the opera and a reservation for dinner at her favorite restaurant. You found Lupita in her pajamas and a mud mask, gathered with all of her family around the TV, watching the final episode of a *telenovela*, surrounded by empty beer bottles, pizza boxes, and the used Kleenexes of a dozen aunts and grandmas.

4. To whom . . . did you think you were getting married?

To a woman? You were wrong, and it shouldn't have taken you ten years to discover it: When a man chooses a Latina as a wife, he's marrying not one girl but the whole family, plus her friends, neighbors, and acquaintances. They'll live together, they'll go on vacations together, if one gets sick, all of them get sick. They tell each other everything, and what's not told is found out, and what's not found out is spied, and what's not spied is "sensed," and what's not "sensed" is fabricated.

THE RIGHT MOMENT TO DELIVER THE NEWS.

Timing is everything. First, hide anything sharp, serrated, or pointy. The most important thing to remember is to fill everything you say with deep feelings and fraught emotions. Remember that Latinas love soap operas, where the most obvious things are said in convoluted sentences employing as many metaphors and adjectives and clichés as linguistically possible. The following are a few examples of how you must translate your English into something more acceptable to the ear of a Latina raised on *telenovelas*:

- I want a divorce: "Like the moon, the brightness of my soul only conceals the darkness behind it, and that shadow will consume it night by night until it is only a sliver, and then only blackness. I must leave now, while scant illumination still permits me to look upon your beautiful face, and remember it like this forever."

- I'm bored with your company: "We laughed like innocent children and tumbled in the tall grass, feeling the warm sunlight on our skin until dusk. But as night passed, a cold fog enveloped us like a blanket and tucked us in for a long, muted slumber, in which we have been haunted by remote memories of lost dreams."

- It's been a while since I last enjoyed sex: "The pure white sheets wrapped around your girlish figure when you, giggling, tried in vain to avoid my kisses, only to surrender ultimately to the wild passion as a love goddess . . . they are now but a clothesline rag, frayed by the icy winds of time and cruel fate, kissed only by dust."

- I'll give you the house, the car, and half the money: "When we were lost in the desert sands and parched, and we thought we would soon be husks for vultures to fight over, we came upon a golden oasis that poured blessings into our cups. That fountain will be yours until the end of time, and even if the desert calls me back into its barren embrace, I will take with me only my own empty cup."

After listening to you speaking this insane nonsense, she'll miraculously get the message, and believe it or not, she'll receive it peacefully, with a kind of sagelike calmness. But if you ignore my advice and speak plainly, she'll be the one providing the insane nonsense—kicking, yelling, cursing, and scratching the police as they try to pull her off you.

GETTING SUSPICION OUT OF YOUR WIFE'S MIND.

Once Lupita has learned the news and accepted it, that doesn't mean everything is going to run smoothly from this point forward. Lupita suspects there are secret reasons behind your desire for a divorce. Some of the most common are:

- That you have another woman. The first and the most obvious possibility, though perhaps the least factual. Be prepared to have your pockets thoroughly rummaged, as well as wallets, cell phones, address books, etc. Don't worry about your e-mail, Lupita won't bother to learn how to turn on the computer.

- That you're gay. It's practically inconceivable for a woman like her, who has so much "flavor"— although after ten years it's a slightly sour flavor—that you could not be having an affair and still not want her. You must be gay. She'll scrutinize all of your friends, colleagues, and acquaintances. She'll observe all kinds of mannerisms that she decides are suspicious. From there, she'll determine which of them are the homosexuals that have stolen her husband, and then she'll begin plotting her revenge on them—even though you are as straight as Charlie Sheen.

- That you're less than a man. This is the third and most desperate option. After your straight friends have been terrorized for "stealing" you, they will manage to convince her that you are not gay. At this point, she will be running out of satisfactory options. Lupita refuses to believe there is a man she can't satisfy, so she concludes the problem must be your virility. This accusation might hurt your pride, but you should go with it—or else run the risk of her making it true, with a steak knife.

FROM DENIAL TO ULTIMATE ACCEPTANCE.

Finally, you've not only made your decision, you've also delivered the news and have stoically borne the subsequent interrogation. If you're still in one piece at this point, you have angels guarding you, that's for sure. Hopefully, they'll keep guarding you, because you'll never again walk down the street completely at ease, because Lupita's brother is in a gang. Every night, you'll have trouble falling asleep, fearing that somebody has hidden a homemade explosive device within your bachelor apartment while you were at work. But these are inevitable, collateral damages.

Before we finish this topic, I want to give you a gift. Perhaps some nights you'll feel remorse, thinking about how much you put poor Lupita through. You could feel guilt, and you might question the decisions you made. Let's be honest, Lupita wasn't that bad of a woman after all. It was never your intention to make her sad and blue, wandering around her mother's house in mourning. Well, I have good news, and that's my present to you: Lupita is not depressed. Not only that, after the divorce she lost weight, she got new boobs, a Botox procedure, and she looks hotter than ever. They always do that. It's their sweet revenge.

Latino women have developed a psychological mechanism that allows them not just to change their mind after a disappointing outcome but to switch realities immediately and completely. When you two were married, everything was wonderful, life was just perfect, and she couldn't have asked for anything more. The day of the divorce, all of her memories changed, and everything switched to the new reality:

Married: You're an American citizen, and you helped her get citizenship.

Divorced: You're a capitalist pig, and you exploited her immigration problems.

Married: You are tall and fit, with a strong hairline.

Divorced: You are vain like a woman, and not man enough to go bald or carry a gut.

Married: Our home is a temple.

Divorced: I'm going to demolish this dump if it doesn't sell soon.

Married: You are a well-educated lawyer, and you provide a nice living for your family.

Divorced: You are a snake who profits from setting murderers free on the streets.

Married: My life is meaningless without you.

Divorced: I hope all your teeth fall out but one, and that one gets a cavity.

CHAPTER 14

TEST #1—LIVING LA VIDA LOCA

Before the end of this part, I must test your Latino-ness. By that I mean how much of the Latino mind-set you've adopted into your system by reading this book. Don't get scared, it's a win-win situation. If you succeed, you'll feel great. If you fail, you'll still have all the money. Try to answer these multiple-choice questions by thinking with a Latino mind. To score, just give yourself 0 points for each "a," 1 point for each "b," and 3 points for each "c" answer.

1. There's somebody at your door. When you open it, you find a woman with a teenaged boy. She says, "This is your son." What's the first thing that comes out of your mouth?
   a. "My lawyer will call you."
   b. "It's impossible, my doctor says I can't have kids."
   c. "Come on in, son, meet your seventeen siblings!"

2. A very good friend chooses you as his best man
   for his wedding. What's your reaction?
   a. You hug him and both cry with happiness together.
   b. You ask, "Do I have to pay for a suit?"
   c. You realize, *Obviously he has no clue that I slept with
   the bride.*

3. Your mother has been found guilty of murder.
   She killed the landlord after a heated argument
   about the rent.
   a. "I love her, but she has to pay her debt to society."
   b. "She was framed!"
   c. "Who isn't six months behind on rent payments?
   He should have minded his own business."

4. Complete the phrase: "When I travel, I like to . . ."
   a. ". . . be in good company."
   b. ". . . ask for a loan to bring the whole family with me."
   c. ". . . ride in the car rather than in the trunk."

5. You are a Latina girl from the barrio (the 'hood).
   One day, while you're waiting at the bus stop, a
   man passes by and caresses your rear end. What's
   your reaction?
   a. You run home, crying the whole way.
   b. You yell "pervert!" at top of your lungs while repeatedly hitting him with your purse.
   c. You cut the man's face up with the razor blade you
   keep under your wig, then you retouch your makeup
   and catch a cab before the police arrive.

Results:

0 to 5 points: You are a logical, objective, and analytical decision maker. You have a long way to go, my friend. You are so preoccupied with protecting the borders of your framework that you don't see the big picture. In fact, you don't see the picture at all. It's a picture of us slowly taking over.

6 to 12 points: You are in the middle. Not too bad, but not too good, either. You have to commit to a decision now and stick to it for the rest of our journey together: Are you willing to dedicate yourself?

13 to 15 points: If you scored 13 points, it means four "c" answers and one "b." How well do you deal with not being perfect? Go back and review the test, you are almost there. If you scored the "perfect 15," you should be very proud of yourself.

PART 2
CULTURE AND PEOPLE

CHAPTER 15

FOOD AMONG LATINOS

Countries can be distinguished not only by the taste of their food but also by their people's eating habits. Within many Latino territories, lunch, known as *el almuerzo*, is usually the main meal of the day. Among the poorer Latinos, it can also be called *la única* (the one) because it is the only meal of the day.

In Latin American countries, adults as well as children take a break from work and school and gather at home to have lunch together. This customary ritual can take up to two hours of our time! Does this information seem incredible to you? I mean the part about adults working and children attending school.

Around five o'clock in the afternoon, it's time for *la merienda*, a light snack of milk and sandwiches. Generally this meal is for children, while they're watching cartoons on TV.

At night, it's time for *la cena*, the dinner, always around nine p.m., extremely late for American customs but quite normal for Latin America. The first time I attended a business dinner in Los Angeles, we ate at five thirty. I got back home at nine, just in time to have real dinner.

When Latinos immigrate, our eating habits change a lot. Apparently we tend to eat less once we're living in the United States. Why is that? There have been many studies conducted on that matter. Philosophers, nutritionists, and psychologists have worked to find an answer. Until recently, there were three main theories regarding the matter:

Theory #1: American food tastes unfamiliar.

Theory #2: Missing your country makes you lose your appetite.

Theory #3: Latinos don't understand food labels written in English.

All three theories were disproved once someone got the idea to ask a Latino. Turns out it's because the food is expensive.

THE THREE BIG TRUTHS ABOUT LATINO CUISINE.

Within any culture, but especially in the Latino world, food represents the culture's identity and traditions. A fondness for typical dishes is one of these things that don't change just because we move out of our countries. It is a way to stay connected with the land in which we grew up. My grandmother always used to say food is first consumed with the eyes, and now I remember her every time I blind myself by splattering ketchup. But of course, that is only the beginning, and the other four senses are involved as well: There's the smell as we sniff the delicious aroma of cooking, the taste when we steal a little morsel from the pot, the sound of the cook screaming "wait until it's ready!" and the touch experience when she smacks your hand with a wooden spoon.

Truth #1: You can smell Latino cooking a mile away. If you have to pass by a Latino restaurant on your way to work or school, you know exactly what I mean. So do your coworkers, since they can smell it on your clothes all the way in the conference room, even though you're still parking your car outside. That smell is a promise of intense flavor, and Latino food is incredibly tasty because of the mix of different ingredients and flavors: something sweet, something salty, and something spicy, all marinated in lime juice and garlic, then fried in pork fat. How do the poorer Latinos manage to survive? They do it following this recipe with whatever they can get their hands on. You could give a tractor tire that treatment and it would be scrumptious. "Necessity is the mother of all invention," my grandmother used to say. You thought the dish *ropa vieja* (old clothes) was a metaphor?

Cristián de la Fuente

Everybody asks me what I do to have a healthy body. Exercise, eight hours of sleep, and a balanced diet . . . except when a good friend comes over.

Truth #2: Latino food is spicy.

Somebody said to me the other day that this is a myth, since not *all* Latino food is spicy. It's true, but the myth persists. Why? Well, let me ask you this: Can I dance? No, I can't, but the majority of Latinos do shine on the dance floor. Because of this reputation, millions of Americans actually thought *I could dance.* They were wrong, but the belief remained. Of course, you can come across some Latino dish that's not spicy, but most are, and the reputation sticks.

Who hasn't seen cartoon characters on TV tasting Latino food and running around with flames coming out of their mouths, then plunging their heads into buckets of water? If you're not used to this kind of heat, it's understandable that you'll have a bad reaction to it—though hopefully not so bad that you have to submerge your head. If you're not a fan of hot food, you might be wondering what the attraction is. My research has taught me that chili peppers have a chemical called capsaicin, which causes pain receptor cells located throughout the mouth, nose, and throat to signal the brain. The brain releases endorphins, the body's natural painkiller. Endorphins soothe the pain, but at the same time they create a temporary feeling of euphoria, not unlike some prescription painkillers. Other side effects are increased heart rate, more salivation, and your intestines gearing up to high speed. To duplicate all of these effects otherwise, you would require morphine, cocaine, castor oil, and rabies. It almost makes the cartoons look like an understatement.

Truth #3: On a Latino dinner table, there's always lots of food. Latinos are always afraid that the food is not going to be enough. If there's an unwritten law on Latino cuisine, it would be: When you cook, cook as if for an entire army. I happen to know about a typical case, in which a man named Ramón Fernández invited his fiancée to an intimate lunch at his mother's house. Ms. Fernandez, who had been a widow for two years, did the math, and she felt that for the three of them it would be appropriate to cook *a whole cow*. She arrived at this conclusion knowing full well that her son's fiancée was a vegetarian.

In what appears to be one of the most amazing paradoxes of the Latino experience, regardless of the income of any family, even one in complete poverty, the food is always plentiful. Perhaps you've heard the expression "Where two can eat, they can accommodate a third." In Latino culture, it's reversed and multiplied by twenty-six.

CHAPTER 16

The Latino Dress Code

Out of all the defining characteristics of Latinos, our taste in clothes is one of the most distinctive. No matter what country we are from, as soon as we arrive in the United States, we seem to be drawn toward certain colors and patterns. I've come to view it as a disease that cures itself after three generations in this country.

The big myth: Latinos can't resist crazy, bright, and neon colors.

The truth is that it's just Latinos from some particular places in the Caribbean. Why those cherry reds, parrot greens, electric blues, gold and silver . . . all in a single jacket? One theory is that these bright colors attract attention, as a way of saying: "Here I am!" That theory makes no sense, however, because being an individual from another country, not speaking a single word in English, and often residing illegally in the United States, the *last* thing you want to do is attract attention. I'm forced to conclude it is a disease, like a Tourette's syndrome for fashion.

You might be thinking, "Who are you fooling, Cristián? We

saw you on *Dancing with the Stars!*" Okay, I never asked for that wardrobe. Every week, I'd go to the dressing room to find another *bright* surprise. I can picture the meetings in the costume design department:

"Let's see, for Priscilla Presley . . . a long black dress?" All nod in agreement.

"Jason Taylor, a big NFL star . . . a light brown suit?" Done and done.

"Cristián de la Fuente . . . pink leather pants, a green jacket, no shirt, and a silver cape?" A round of light applause. And to think I was dancing the Viennese waltz that week. I began to think this situation over. It's true we Latinos have bright spirits, colorful personalities, and crazy determination. However, that doesn't mean our outfits need to be bright, colorful, and crazy. I decided to approach the show's costume designer to discuss my concern. Before I could meet with him, people started voting for me. I realized they probably voted for me because they *noticed* me. I decided to shut my mouth, and I was amazed to see myself and my crazy outfits staying in the competition week after week.

In my case, the Latino fashion myth helped me succeed in my job. We can concede that, for certain professions, these brightly colored clothes can come in handy. Here are some examples of extreme Latino fashion and the specific jobs in which it is actually helpful:

• **The "Tropical."** You know the kind of look I'm talking about. A mosaic of jungle green, papaya red, sky blue, and cosmic orange. Maybe even a touch of yellow—for instance, the shoes. This look is perfect for bartenders, travel agents, salsa dance instructors, time-share salesmen, gigolos, movie producers, or anyone else who wants to create an exotic, fantasy atmosphere.

- **The "Terminator."** This is the tough guy with the gold jacket and the silver pants. He's an ideal candidate to sell sunglasses, partly because he looks like a cool and dangerous robot sent from the future, and partly because his outfit necessitates them for everyone around him.

- **The "Patriot."** This look is achieved by combining the colors of your clothes to resemble your country's flag. I'm as patriotic as anybody, but flags were made to fly as a single piece of fabric, tied to a pole. If you were born in Brazil, please tell me that in a way other than wearing green pants, a yellow shirt, and a blue hat. Don't get me wrong, it's fine to pin a flag to your jacket or cap. But combining different-colored clothes to resemble a human flag is a look only fit for a circus performer—hopefully one with man-eating lions that are attracted to bright colors.

CHAPTER 17

Latino Gangs

I'm going to take this opportunity to shed some light on what would probably be the biggest myth about Latinos: that we're all in gangs. I've appeared on TV, dancing the cha-cha in a pink suit. Honestly, how do you see that working out with my violent street organization? Do you think I left the studio and helped my boys do a drive-by?

I understand, you are afraid that your daughter is going to end up dating one of the members of this tiny minority who have helped to perpetuate this awful myth. Don't worry, she could do a lot worse. She could date a lawyer.

Let's do an exercise to try to get some knowledge about gangs. I'll write a statement and you will think whether it's true or false. Are you ready?

- Latinos left their countries dreaming about a better future in North America.
  Yes, that's true.

- They left an insecure place, with a devastated economy and almost no chances for their kids to succeed in life.
  Of course, that's also true.
- Latino gangs' fights are mostly about territory.
  That's true.
- So, they wear pink suits to dance the cha-cha on the streets of the barrio.
  I'm sorry. I'm messing with you. I just wanted to see if you were paying attention.

At the end of the day, you need to be able to differentiate between a gang member and a regular Latino guy who's just hanging around the neighborhood. Let me start by saying that this is no exact science. There are some gray zones here and there. I realize that you probably don't spend too much time in gang-infested neighborhoods, so how can you have a point of reference? Now, obviously I'm not going to send you into a dangerous area. After all, you bought my book, and I am indebted to you. There is a place that you can observe dangerous beasts without risk of life and limb, and it's called the zoo. So, let's tour the zoo and learn what we can about gangs.

- **The wolf cage.** A wolf marks his territory by peeing in specific places, so the other wolves know that spot belongs to him. But the wolf is no fool. He knows that the territory is only his until a bigger predator claims it. It's the same thing with Latino gangs: they pee on their streets, and they don't like others peeing there. However, they're not as smart as wolves. They truly believe they own the territory, when in fact it always belongs to a bigger predator: the police.

• **The monkey cage.** We have all witnessed a sunny Saturday family outing to the zoo go suddenly wrong due to a lewd and embarrassing scene inside the monkey cage. As the otherwise adorable primates showboat their junk to the ladies, Dad turns and marches everybody directly to the hippopotamus pond. Same thing happens with Latino gangs. If you walk by a bunch of them with your family, they will proudly rub their crotches, or else they'll try to touch your teenage daughter (or wife, or grandma), as you hurriedly drag your family to a safer place, like an illegal poker den or a crack house.

• **The lion cage.** Why is it that the lion is king? He's big and strong, but there certainly are bigger, stronger, and faster animals than him. The lion is king because of his roar. The louder the roar, the more powerful the lion. Same thing with Latino gangs. They let their motorcycles rumble for hours in front of your house, as noisily as they can, in an effort to prove themselves kings of the road. I suggest you do the same as the other animals in the zoo—ignore the meaningless racket and go about your business.

• **The cheetah cage.** The cheetah is the fastest land mammal on the face of the earth, reaching seventy miles per hour at top speed. They can only keep that pace for four hundred to six hundred yards, then they get exhausted and are at the mercy of other predators. The same thing happens with Latino gang members. They live at a sprint, but they are quickly exhausted and vulnerable to predators—for example, their own girlfriends, who easily chase them down, marry them, and domesticate them into harmless house pets.

CHAPTER 18

Latino Stereotypes

Since the beginning of time, humans have tried to make sense of the world. One tactic is to separate people into several groups, labeling them based on age, gender, religion, economic status, political inclinations, sexual preferences, or ethnic backgrounds. We are individuals, but we also belong to a number of groups. Once we are neatly categorized, the temptation is to observe some kind of inherent traits or patterns—if not, what's the point of categorization in the first place? For instance, there is a popular myth that black men are especially well endowed. Is it true or not? Can we generalize? We all have our doubts on the matter—except for black men, of course. If Chileans had that reputation, I wouldn't exactly go around denying it, either. These myths about other groups' traits originate in the interactions between two or more members of different groups. That's where the tall tales begin. Following the previous example, if a black woman only dates black men, she's not going to be able to draw a comparison. If she dates men with a variety of ethnicities, she will be able to confirm or deny the stereotype, at least in her own experience. Despite society's efforts to keep us all separated, the temptation to cross group lines is too strong to resist, and by now everybody has experienced the quirks of the other groups, or at least has heard about them secondhand.

When we step into the Latino world, there are many myths and stereotypes. After decades of oral tradition and hearsay, I guess it's about time to write some of them down, explain their origins, and weigh their validity. After an intensive compilation of data and comprehensive interviews, I've pared countless rumors down to five main stereotypes. But just how accurate are they?

Stereotype #1: Latinos are more sexually passionate.
I've analyzed a specific case through the testimony of Jenny Bates, a fifty-two-year-old from El Paso, Texas, who recalled her affair with her Latino gardener in a series of letters to a local newspaper. In these letters, she chronicles her "meetings" with Antonio Mendez, then thirty-four years old, a Peruvian living in the United States for the last two years. This is a brief excerpt from one of those letters: "After he came into the house, he took five minutes to close and lock all doors and windows, he ripped my clothes off and jumped over the bed, he dragged me to the bathroom, later to the basement, and even behind the fridge. He was so hot." This account could be evidence supporting the stereotype. However, she later discovered that Antonio was an illegal immigrant running from El Paso Border Patrol agents. His creative use of locations during lovemaking turned out to be a constant search for a place to hide from authorities. Since then, Jenny and Antonio have married and live in Mexico. Now that nobody is chasing him, she complains he's not as hot as he used to be.

Stereotype #2: Latinos accept jobs we wouldn't take back home. This is absolutely true. I personally know a lot of people who wouldn't wait tables at a restaurant back in their countries, but nonetheless they willingly take the job as immigrants. This happens for a lot of reasons. First, most Latin American countries don't have restaurants—kidding! But seriously, here a full-time waiter has enough money to pay the rent, lease a car, feed his family, and even educate his children. In Latin America, a full-time waiter makes barely enough money to pay the bus fare to and from his job.

As in many other situations in life, it's not the prestige of the job that counts, it's the paycheck. Some extremists have said that given the right amount of money, human beings are capable of almost anything. Then the TV show *Fear Factor* demonstrated that they are not extremists. The Latino agrees to do basically any job, so long as the pay allows him to live a decent life. When he visits his home country, he would probably hide some details about the way he makes a living in the United States. For instance, he might drop hints about his gig at NASA headquarters, but he'll probably leave out that his job is to empty the zero-gravity toilets. As my dad used to say: "Everybody has a price." Those who say they don't are only more expensive.

Stereotype #3: Latinos keep to themselves.
This myth is completely and definitively false. There's nothing a Latino could wish for more than to interact with his fellow Americans. Bill Gates's Latino caddie has invited him over to his house several times to share arroz con pollo (rice with chicken) and to discuss the future of robots. Ramon, Donald Trump's limo driver, is tired of trying to convince the mogul to join him for drinks at a Dominican bar in Inwood. Rita Cortese, a housekeeper in one of Barbra Streisand's mansions, has prepared pop-

corn and martinis many times for her boss, but is still waiting for an invitation to give her opinion about *Meet the Fockers* (Hilarious!). When we ended filming *Basic,* I invited John Travolta to my house. I guess he never showed up because I don't have an airport runway in my backyard. Latinos would love to mix with Americans, but it's going to take some time.

Stereotype #4: Latino women are game for love.

This can be true, but you have to understand it's highly situational. Picture this: Mexico, DF. A young woman named Maria is on the curb waiting for *la guagua* (the bus) to go back home after eight hours of working in a Mexican hat factory. Suddenly, a mud-caked car comes to a screeching halt right in front of her. A man with a wide mustache who smells of whiskey and wet dog says, "*¿Pa'donde mi reina?* [Burp!]," which means "Where are you heading to, girl? [Burp!]" Maria rejects him gently, even though she'd walk to New York before getting in the car with him. After begging her forty-two more times, the man realizes his chances to score are below zero, so he starts the car again—which takes several attempts—and drives off to the closest bar, which luckily for him is only a few feet away.

Now picture this. Los Angeles, California. A young woman named Maria is at the curb waiting for *la guagua* (the bus) to go

Here we are in Chile, celebrating my daughter's third birthday with our closest family members. Just some Latino cousins. Can you find me in the picture?

Cristián de la Fuente

back home after eight hours of working at a fast-food restaurant. Suddenly, a car—or something so dazzlingly bright that it could be a spaceship—hits the brakes right in front of her. A fit, well-groomed man who smells of expensive cologne whispers suggestively, "You need a ride, *mamacita?*" Maria swoons into the backseat of the car and says they can go anywhere and do anything. Are you ready for the big twist? This is the *same Maria* as in the first example! So is it true that she was game for love? Well, that kind of depends on a lot of things.

Stereotype #5: Latino families are too big.

This is true, but not for the reason you think. It's not that our families are especially big, it's that our houses are especially small, so that even an average-sized family is too big. There is a related myth that poor Latino families have no TV, so we spend all our time making babies. This is easily disproved by the 2007 writers' strike. *Nobody* watched TV for four months, and yet there wasn't a population explosion, at least not that I know of.

CHAPTER 19

Latino Health Care and the *Curandero*

Faith and trust are a big part of choosing a doctor, or anyone responsible for your health care. They are also an especially critical issue in Latino culture, since we always believe what we want or need to believe, and we can switch our realities back and forth within seconds, depending on the situation.

Let's say we go to the doctor, and he runs a couple of tests. He says everything's fine, and we believe him. If he had said there's something wrong, we would say he doesn't know what he's talking about. We would never go back to a doctor who diagnoses us with an illness, especially one we can't even pronounce. We say: "That can't be right. There has to be someone else to ask." Instead of wasting our time and energy treating only the symptoms of a disease, we spend it looking for a complete cure: the opposite diagnosis.

Truth: Latinos prefer Latino doctors.
Of course, I'm talking about only those lucky Latinos who can afford health insurance. We go through the directory looking for familiar last names like González or Gómez. We feel much im-

proved just for having found a doctor named Pérez. Sometimes, when we can't find any Latino specialists, we don't make an appointment at all. We'll say, "If I'm going to die, I want somebody to tell me in Spanish, or not at all."

In Latin America, proper health care is a luxury. Over there, we have our own version of a health care professional, and we have brought him with us to the United States. He will tell us the most inconceivable reasons for an illness . . . and we believe him, because it's not a logical diagnosis that can be debated, it's the mysterious insight of an omniscient force that speaks through him. Let me introduce you to the *curandero*, the Latin American folk healer. A *curandero* is a man (or a woman, in which case she's called *curandera*) who has a direct line with healing spirits that are willing to tell us how to cure what ails us.

Myth: *Curanderos* can cure illnesses doctors are clueless about. The myth is not the part about doctors being clueless about some illnesses, that's completely true. The myth is that a *curandero* can cure even perfectly curable ailments, much less incurable ones. While Latinos have no problem disputing the advice of a medical doctor, not even an atheist Latino would dare to disregard the advice of his *curandero*. The Harvard-educated doctor who tells us we have syphilis? A quack! The illiterate herdsman who was once struck by lightning and yells at the demons he can see all around us? Not a quack!

To a *curandero*, everything that can possibly be wrong with you is caused by one of three things:

1. bad spirits

2. a lesson from God

3. a curse

The thing is, how do you disagree? Let's say Jose Mendez goes to see a *curandero* because he can't sleep at night. After a series of rituals and ceremonies, he says Jose has floating around his bedroom the angry spirit of a man kidnapped and killed three centuries ago. Jose mentions that in addition to his sleeplessness, a car hit him. Was that the angry spirit's doing? "No, that's God reminding you to take a better look before crossing the street." The *curandero* notices Jose has a black eye. That settles it, Jose is cursed. That's the answer Jose was waiting for! He is cursed and learning a lesson from God and being haunted by an angry spirit. Jose is the victim of many trials, but untested faith is not faith at all. Jose feels much better.

What never gets addressed are the facts, like he got hit crossing the street because he was drunk, and then his wife punched him in the eye for coming home at three a.m., and he couldn't sleep because he spent the rest of the night in the bathroom vomiting whiskey and pretzel sticks. None of this needs to be addressed; so long as he drinks an elixir of dried snail powder, raw eggs, triple-distilled water, and cigar ashes twice a day, he'll be fine. But listen, I'm not here to judge. If you want to believe that a frog peeing over the belly of a pregnant woman can predict the sex of the baby, good for you! Whether or not the sonogram is more accurate, it's not my place to say—but I can tell you it's definitely far less disgusting!

CHAPTER 20

THE MYSTIC LATINO—HOROSCOPES AND SUPERSTITIONS

My great-aunt used to say, "You ought to believe in something." For the last twenty years, she has believed that her husband is still out having a cigarette and could return at any moment. We can learn something from that, besides the fact my great-uncle must smoke very, very slowly. All of mankind feels the urge to believe in something, but Latinos might take it a little further than most.

Truth #1: Latinos believe in magic.
Within the Latino world, everything has certain magical connotations. Generations of turmoil, poverty, and strife have yielded the hope that some kind of supernatural force could change destiny, and that groundless superstitions and rituals can win lady luck's favor. When nothing else is working, you get a little desperate. I mean, what's more feasible—inventing a way to grow crops in barren soil during a drought, or washing the floor with "dragon's blood" and burying a *loteria* card under a full moon?

Truth #2: Latinos love horoscopes.

Even nonbelievers follow their horoscopes. We will base the biggest decisions of our lives on an entertainment feature in a fifty-cent newspaper. The broader the abstraction, the more we feel it applies to us personally. What's this, "Troubles with someone near me"? Hmm, the dog did have a touch of diarrhea, yes. How do they do it, week after week? "Venus's moon enters the sun's fifth house"? Wow! Sounds like the whole solar system moves around to influence my affairs, and something really important is about to happen! I had better pay attention to my "lucky numbers of the day"! For Latinos, fate and destiny trump common sense every time.

Case #1: Four hundred guests packed themselves into a small but cozy church for Alina Gonzalez and Ramon Hermosillo's wedding. Ramon was wearing an impeccable rented black tuxedo. The door opened and the bride walked in, but without her father, and not wearing her wedding dress, and carrying a small suitcase. Weeping, she walked toward the groom, kissed him softly on his cheek, and said: "I have joined NASA. Thus the wedding is postponed until further notice, I'm sorry." That morning, Alina's horoscope had read: "Don't let something black remain by your side. Shoot for the moon and beyond."

Case #2: One summer morning, Maria Gutierrez left the breakfast table, did the dishes, got dressed, walked down the street, turned left, and knocked on a stranger's door. When he answered, she kissed him, pushed her way inside, kicked the door shut, and made love to him for the rest of the day. Her horoscope had read: "Passion is just around the corner."

Case #3: Doctor Juan Gonzalez, an Aries, once read: "You can always find an Aries where the action is; for instance, firefighter is one of their typical job choices." Despite his love for medicine and frail build, he recognized that we cannot change our fate. He quit his job as a respected researcher and has spent the past twelve years training for the physical requirements test for his new profession, which includes a three-mile walk with a forty-five-pound vest, to be completed in under forty-five minutes.

One could argue that all of the more outrageous actions taken by Latinos can be traced back to a horoscope. Here are some historical events, along with the horoscopes that ran that day:

- A record number of Mexicans decide to sneak across the border: *"This new year, your life will have no boundaries."*
- A 500 percent increase in the demand for fake Social Security cards: *"You need to find a new self."*
- A record number of Latinos join gangs: *"Friends will be your source of strength and prosperity."*
- Suddenly, every Latino seems to have three mistresses: *"Your lucky number is 4."*

Horoscopes capture the imaginations of all sorts of people. But only a Latino would say, "Hey, I'm sorry. It's not that I wanted to kiss your wife . . . it was in the horoscope," with the full expectation that his friend will say, "Okay, yes, it was in the horoscope . . .," and that they will continue to be best buddies.

Truth #3: Latinos are superstitious.
Forget about simply avoiding things like black cats, walking under ladders, broken mirrors, or the number thirteen. A Latino believes he's able to manage his good or bad luck and predict, or even change, his own fate by means of concrete actions. Does

this contradict his belief that horoscopes dictate an inescapable fate? Yes, it does. Does that bother him in the slightest? No, it does not.

I'm guilty of superstition myself. When I was competing on *Dancing with the Stars*, I received a lot of gifts from well-intentioned people. Along with cards, blessed candles, and flowers, I got a number of bracelets that I had to wear all the time. One had eyes all around it, another had the image of the Virgin, and one even had Judas Tadeo, "the saint of the impossible," which is not exactly a vote of confidence. But you know, they must have worked, because making it to the finals was a miracle.

One thing that makes our superstitions embarrassing is that they are out of date. We need to develop new, improved, and modern superstitions, more appropriate for this century. The belief that spilling salt is bad luck dates back to the Roman practice of using salt as currency—hence the word "salary." Thirteen is bad luck because Jesus Christ's last meal was twelve apostles and himself, and that was more than two thousand years ago. Let me suggest a couple Latino-friendly superstitions for the twenty-first century, which will surely spread to other cultures in the course of a few years:

- *"It is bad luck to help Immigration Services."* It's good luck to tell them you haven't seen anyone of interest, and that you don't know anything.
- *"Learning English brings bad luck."* It's not that you can't do it or that you don't want to try, it's that you're not crazy enough to tempt fate.
- *"Making love with a Latino man brings good fortune."* Never mind that this has never worked for our wives.
- *"Handing your passport to a family member is bad*

luck." Especially if several of you are in a line, and you're all trying to use it to enter the country.

Managing supernatural forces is a specialty called *hacer un trabajo* (to do a job). This consists of white magic spells, both home-brewed and professionally made. I'm going to share some of the most popular "works" within Latino culture, and believe me, I haven't made up a single one. This kind of information will come in handy if you spend some time around Latinos, so you'll be able to know what our intentions were when you find a dead frog inside your desk drawer.

- **Protecting your home.** To avoid envious people upsetting your home's natural balance, you have to set a glass of salted water behind the front door and change it frequently—for instance, every time your dog knocks it over.
- **Marital harmony.** Take an almond in its shell and write your name on it, then write your beloved's on another one. Carve your wedding date in a white candle and light it beside the almonds. When the candle is totally burned out, break the shells and eat both almonds. Now you understand why Latinas get so fat after they marry: thousands and thousands of almonds.
- **Somebody is bothering you.** You just have to write down his or her name on a piece of paper, fold it in half, and put it in the freezer. This will "freeze" that person, so they won't bother you anymore. You could also kill this person, chop him up, and hide the pieces inside the freezer. Whichever you're more comfortable with.

- **If you have a rival.** Let's say you both are looking for a promotion. You must write down the other person's name on a piece of paper, then put it inside your shoe so you spend all day stepping on your competition. You will never see a Latina buying insoles, because she needs that space to accommodate the names of her many enemies.

CHAPTER 21

LATINO WEIRD CELEBRATIONS

September 18 is Chile's Independence Day, and the next day is the military parade. Those two days are holidays in Chile, and when I can't travel to be there, I don't want to go to work here. I understand that I'm an immigrant now, and I have Thanksgiving and the Fourth of July instead of my country's holidays, but I can't help it—the habit is ingrained from celebrating it all my life. Because I am universally pro-Latino, I also take the day off every Cinco de Mayo (Mexico), Discovery of Puerto Rico Day (Puerto Rico), Lady of Altagracia Day (Dominican Republic), Carnival festival (Cuba), and La Paz Day (El Salvador). It's not that I don't want to work, I do, really—but I don't want to disrespect any of my Latino brothers and sisters!

Let's now analyze how the similarly ingrained celebrations that Latinos may have had back in our countries can emerge years later within our American lives.

"EL DÍA DE LOS MUERTOS" (THE DAY OF THE DEAD).

Observed on November 2 in Mexico, this is a commemoration of the loved ones who have passed away and of the continuation of life itself. It's not a morbid occasion, but rather a festive time. Generalizing broadly, the holiday's activities consist of families: (1) welcoming their dead back into their homes, and (2) visiting the graves of their close kin. At the cemetery, family members engage in sprucing up the grave site, decorating it with flowers, enjoying a picnic, and interacting socially with other families and community members who gather there.

It seems to be a very remarkable celebration the brain must keep memories of somewhere, even when the Mexicans no longer live in their country. Take a look at the similarities: In order to survive in the United States, first-generation immigrants must work themselves to death and come home dead tired. They drop into bed as if it were a grave—meanwhile, their Americanized children, live-in parents and grandparents, and illegal, garage-dwelling cousins party all night long, drinking, eating, playing video games, and watching R-rated movies on Cinemax.

"THE NEW NEW INDEPENDENCE."

Cubans have three independence days: from Spain (October 10, 1868), from the United States (May 20, 1902), and from Cuba (January 1, 1959). They also have to keep track of February 24 (start of the 1895 revolution), March 13 (commemoration of the attack on the Presidential Palace), July 25–27 (commemoration of the storming of the Moncada Barracks), September 28 (anniversary of the Committee for the Defense of the Revolution), October 8 (Che Guevara's anniversary), October 10 (start of the War of Independence), and December 2 (landing of the *Granma* yacht).

Cristián de la Fuente

Every September I do my best to go to Chile to participate in my country's military parade as part of the aerobatic team. Yes, I'm the only one who looks like an actor.

A boss might ask a Cuban-born employee, "Hey, where were you yesterday?"

"Celebrating Independence Day."

"Again? It's the fifth one!"

"And?"

"And what do you take me for?"

"Look it up, jefe, it's legit."

CHAPTER 22

LATINOS AND GAMBLING

Human beings have many ways to achieve our goals and plans: hard work, dedication, intelligence, connections, talent, and perseverance. But not one of these—or even all of them combined—compares to luck. We Latinos are dreamers by nature, so of course we are overly captivated by lady luck . . . and easy marks for her pimp, the one-armed bandito.

Truth #1: Latinos gamble like crazy.
We'll bet on lotto, sports, cockfights, catfights, mud wrestling, thumb wrestling, horse racing, dog racing, cockroach racing, *The Amazing Race*, the arms race, the Race for the Cure, or whatever else you've got. Every single bet is a potential ticket to paradise, the chance to get all those things we fight for every day, only without having to fight.

In the mind of anyone with no money, the idea of becoming a millionaire all of a sudden is an appealing solution—when in fact it's part of the problem. Gamblers aren't discouraged by losing, because their hopeful enthusiasm doesn't disappear right away. It lasts long enough for them to buy the next ticket . . . again, and again, and again.

Once a Latino realizes he's consistently not winning the lotto, usually after fifteen years of playing every day, he starts making what I like to call *avenger bets*. These are bets placed among friends, in the hopes of winning their meager funds, since it's easier to beat a friend than to beat the system. When I started on *Dancing with the Stars*, some Latino fans would approach me, saying: "Listen, I bet a hundred bucks you are in the bottom two this week. Please don't be offended, but could you make sure I don't lose that money?" Or else: "Cristián, I bet my sister that you end up on top this week . . . so how's it going, do you need any tips or pointers?" I also had this awkward conversation:

Monday morning, Los Angeles, on the street:

Guy: Hey, Cristián! How are you? It's me, Ramon, remember?

Me: Hi, yes, yes. (No.)

Guy: I used to mow your lawn in Chile. Long time no see; it's been what . . . ten years?

Me: Feels like less.

Guy: So I watch you on *Dancing with the Stars* every night, it's awesome.

Me: But it's a weekly show!

Guy: Yes, of course, I tape it to watch again and again. I bet you make it to the finals.

Me: Thank you, I'll do my best.

Guy: No, seriously, I've bet two weeks' salary with my cousin. He thinks Mario is going to beat you.

Me: Well, I have to go.

Guy: (Grabbing my arm) You are going to make it, right?

Do you need me to mow your lawn tomorrow? Would that help you?

Me: I live in an apartment now, but thank you.

Guy: You should be rehearsing rather than wasting time walking in the street.

Me: I'm going to the doctor. I injured my arm last night. Did you see the show?

Guy: Err, of course, yes. Excuse me, I have to call someone (dialing).

Me: I can still dance, you know?

Guy: Of course (waving me off). Manuel? Ah, listen . . .

Me: Okay, I guess I'll just be going then.

If I may, I have a personal message to Ramon: You would've won that bet, and I still don't remember who the hell you are.

Truth #2: Gambling addiction is not acquired at the border. One reason Latinos tend to gamble is that our home countries had weak economies and few real opportunities. If U.S. Latinos are dreamers, those living in Latin America are the walking comatose. Over there, lottery marketing is aggressive and practically impossible to resist. The following are lottery advertising slogans you could find in different countries across Latin America. I promise I didn't make any of them up:

- "Live your dreams!" (Honduras)
  Only if you win, of course. Otherwise, "dream your life."
- "The one who gives the most money out!" (Colombia)
  Compared to . . . the other Colombian lottery?
- "We work making dreams come true." (Mexico)
  . . . dreams of not working.

- "We all win." (Puerto Rico)
  But we don't all collect.
- "Your Lottery." (Venezuela)
  Just not your money.
- "You play, we don't." (Argentina)
  We're not going to steal the pot this time.

Personally, I think that even though those ads are aggressive, they could step it up. "Live your dreams" is very soft in today's competitive advertising landscape. People would bet a lot more if the ad spoke directly to them, for example:

- "Do you want to die poor and alone?"
- "What did you think, hard work would be rewarded?"
- "With your looks, you'd better get rich."
- "Buy the company and fire your boss."
- "Buy the country and fire the government."

When Fidel Castro took over Cuba's government in 1959, he abolished the National Lottery of Cuba. Nevertheless, there is still plenty of gambling going on under the radar, and some have been known to give this advice: *"A bet is 50 percent that you'll lose your money, but Fidel is 100 percent."*

Truth #3: Latinos see winning a bet as a life achievement. Living in a society that seems so intent on keeping us from being winners, Latinos crave the feeling of beating the odds at something. We don't even have to win millions of dollars, just the sensation of overcoming the competition can be enough. Even old-fashioned town fair–type competitions, like "guess my age" or "guess my weight," can give the feeling of "I won."

114

Recently, I read about a betting house in London, England, that accepts any kind of wager you're able to come up with and put money on. You could show up there saying that a man will step on Mars before 2020. The house analyzes the likelihood and takes your bet, giving you the odds they've calculated—1 in 10 or 1 in 1,000 or 1 in 1,000,000—take it or leave it. When I learned about this house and its tremendous success, I couldn't help but think about how they would do targeting the Latino market.

The first thing to contend with is that nothing is simple with Latinos. Back in London, you might get "I bet my mother lives to a hundred years old." When a Latino places the same bet, it looks like this: "I bet my mother, who's really my ex-stepmother since she divorced a man who beat the hell out of her to marry my father, but then went back to him, but then he died of heart disease, is going to live—if you could call that a life, being the cleaning lady of wealthy people who mistreat her and sleeping in the same bed with my ex-step-grandmother because she has no bed of her own, with no air-conditioning, is going to reach fifty-five years of age, but that she'll complain of feeling like she's a hundred and fifty, and will insist that both she and her mother are entitled to live in my house for free because we are family." By the time the bet is finally written down, the mother will be dead already.

I believe betting on numbers is dull, it's too abstract. Let me propose right now some new games of chance:

DAILY DERBY GOLD RUSH

A hundred Latinos get ready near a U.S. border. At a given signal, everybody runs to American territory while being chased by ten law enforcement officials. You could bet on how many of them make it to the other side without being caught. Seems too cruel to you? Keep in mind that it's actually happening already, we're just not betting on it . . . yet. Okay, to make you feel better, we could arrange to donate part of the earnings to some foundation that helps immigrants . . . let's say 5 percent? After taxes and my fee, of course (I did think of the idea, be reasonable).

FANTASY 12 POWER PICK

An inner-city Latino newborn is secretly selected at random. You buy a ticket for $5, and the value triples for every grade he completes in school. There's a lot working against him—poverty, racism, violence, drugs all around, not to mention an older girlfriend who keeps "accidentally" forgetting to take her birth control. But if he can hang in there for twelve grades, you get $2.65 million. When the minor reaches legal age, he'll get a share of the money, which could be used to finish his education, or to buy a custom iced-out grill from Paul Wall.

HOT SPOT QUICK DRAW

We monitor an anonymous individual between eighteen and sixty years old, taking bets on how many times in one year he or she falls into a hot, passionate Latin love affair. Cousins, same-sex experimentation, and professional services don't count. The strategy here would be like keno—while you can't improve the chances that your guess is right, you can minimize the chances of having to share the pot by picking a seemingly unlikely number, like 0 or 200.

Truth #4: Gamblers Anonymous doesn't work for Latinos.

Fidel Castro once said, "Any excess is bad." Maybe after a hundred years in power, he'll see the irony of that statement. Of course, it's true that anything can be bad if overindulged, and not just tangible things like food and alcohol, but also behaviors like sex and gambling. With this truth in mind, Gamblers Anonymous was founded in 1957 to gather gamblers together and help them fight their addiction using the world-famous 12-step method. That's just not going to work for us. Let me ask you, have you not seen the Pyramid of the Sun at Teotihuacan? 248 steps. That is how we do it; we're not trying to sprain an ankle getting somewhere in just 12 steps. If you want to make a 248-step recovery program, you might get some traction with Latinos, otherwise forget it.

The following questionnaire will help you determine whether your Latino friend/acquaintance/neighbor has a gambling problem. If he answers "yes" to at least three of the questions, consider it a red flag:

1. Did you ever sell personal belongings to get gambling money?

2. Were any of those your children?

3. Has gambling ruined your reputation?

4. Is that because your reputation was already bad?

5. Has gambling ever made your wife unhappy?

6. Does everything make your wife unhappy?

7. Have creditors or loan sharks ever shown up at your door?

8. Have your creditors and loan sharks ever gotten into a rumble on your front lawn?

9. Have you ever gambled as a way to dodge answers? Cut it out right now and answer this!

10. Do you understand that "gambling" is the English word for *apostar*?

11. Is there a reason you waited until the tenth question to tell me you don't speak English?

12. Is it because you were betting I wouldn't notice?

CHAPTER 23

Latino Facts and Statistics

I know it's too much for me to ask for you to believe everything I say about Latinos simply because you bought this book. As a respectable author, I should research information and tangible facts, as well as revealing numbers and statistics. All right, I'll keep any speculation contained to my brief commentary on each of the following facts, which are otherwise absolutely true.

The top five largest Latino-populated cities in the United States are: Los Angeles, San Francisco, Miami, New York, and Chicago. Two on each coast and one in the middle of the country . . . does this strike anyone else as less like a random distribution pattern and more like a calculated invasion with several strategic fronts?

The Census Bureau has estimated that before 2020, one out of five Americans will be Latino. What they left out is that he will be one of your five children, and your wife will pretend you're talking nonsense.

In 2007, Marvel Comics launched a new all-Latino superhero team called the Santerians where its main character is transformed into his superhero alter ego Eleggua after an Afro-Caribbean Santeria ceremony. They put chicken blood in the ink—if you browse the comic without buying it, you will be cursed with social awkwardness and virginity forever.

On average, Anglos take 33.24 minutes to make love, including foreplay. The average woman says she could use a good 12 extra minutes. Latinos, on the other hand, take 180 minutes to make love (granted, we also stop in the middle to go to the fridge and grab a beer), yet our wives say they could use a good 12 extra minutes. Then there are the tantric yogis of Tibet: they go for 36 hours, yet their wives say they could use a good 12 extra minutes.

Until 1999, it was legal to marry a fourteen-year-old woman in Utah. Latinos think it's still legal, and that California, New York, and Florida are all part of Utah.

Immigration experts say a growing number of migrants who have toiled in the United States as laborers, janitors, and car mechanics are being recruited to run for office in their home countries. In politics, it certainly can't hurt to have experience getting rid of garbage.

Seventy-three percent of U.S. Latinos consulted by a poll say we avoid retirement because we're afraid we won't have enough money to survive. True, but 90 percent of us don't make enough money to survive *before* retirement.

The parents from the North Little Rock Public Education Foundation did some research and found that when it comes to introducing new language skills, the earlier the better. So they designed a Spanish pilot program for a group of young students under ten years old. In a related report, 95 percent of the girls attending the program dropped out because they didn't want to miss the *novelas* on TV every afternoon.

According to the National Association of Hispanic Journalists, from the approximately 16,000 stories broadcast by TV news shows (ABC, CBS, NBC, and CNN) they reviewed throughout 2001, only 99 of them were about Latinos. They could have just said 2001 was a slow year for illegal immigration and crimes of passion.

In 1968, the U.S. Congress authorized then President Lyndon B. Johnson to proclaim seven days during September as the "National Week of Hispanic Patriotism." The celebration was extended to last one month long in 1988 (from September 15 to October 15). Seemingly, seven days were not enough for Latinos to recover from our massive, patriotic hangovers.

By the year 2050, researchers say the number of Latinos with Alzheimer's will increase by 600 percent. I say they won't really have the disease; they will fake having lost their memories so they can pass as Anglos: "My name is Jasper Worthington, from Connecticut originally, so nice to meet you."

In May 2007, Mexico City's Vive Latino Latin Rock festival reportedly topped box-office charts in North America for the first week of the month, grossing $2.5 million and selling 107,000 tickets. Given the special talent Latinos have at finding ways to get into venues for free, I'd put the actual attendance at around 250,000.

The U.S. Census Bureau stated that in 2003, 92.5 percent of the foreigners in the civilian labor force were employed. What the study didn't state is that because 45 percent of us had called in sick and another 45 percent were suing our employers for discrimination, only 2.5 percent were actually working.

In 2002, 26.5 percent of Latino family households consisted of five or more people. Ha, ha, ha! Learn how to look in the garage, in the closet, and under the bed. Believe me, 100 percent of Latino family households consisted of five or more people.

CHAPTER 24

DIFFERENCES BETWEEN ANGLOS AND LATINOS, PART 2

Now it's time to take what we've learned about Latino culture in this section and observe it in practice—the extreme situations that destiny sometimes puts on our paths. Let us acknowledge our similarities, but also celebrate our differences.

- *Situation A.* You walk into a bar to meet with some old high school buddies. Some of them are married, and their wives are there. Nobody told you any specifics about the attire, but everybody looks like they're about to attend a wedding. You, on the other hand, are wearing a golf shirt and madras shorts. What do you do?
  - **Underdressed Anglo:** Before anybody notices his presence, checks his watch to see if there's enough time to go home and change.
  - **Underdressed Latino:** Pops his collar for a fashion-boost.

- **Underdressed Anglo:** Nervously jokes, "Hey, guys, who's getting married?"
- **Underdressed Latino:** Grabs a buddy and rubs his face in his armpit until everybody laughs.
- **Underdressed Anglo:** Says, "I'm sorry, I forgot to ask what to wear."
- **Underdressed Latino:** Says, "I think of the macaw as God's fashion ambassador."
- *Situation B.* You're in a full elevator. You just finished lunch, and you feel something bad going on in your stomach. Right after the elevator door closes, you can't hold it anymore—you pass gas loudly, and it stinks in there. How do you handle the situation?
  - **Gassy Anglo:** Starts coughing to cover the sound.
  - **Gassy Latino:** Asks, "Did somebody step on a duck or what?"
  - **Gassy Anglo:** Says, "Excuse me, I apologize, I have a medical digestive condition."
  - **Gassy Latino:** Says, "Whoa, you can smell the garlic in that!"
  - **Gassy Anglo:** Gets out on the next floor, even though it's not where he was headed.
  - **Gassy Latino:** Does not get out on the next floor, even though it was where he was headed.
- *Situation C.* You witness a huge car accident two blocks from your house, with cars piled up everywhere. What do you do?
  - **Anglo witness:** Calls 911 on her cell phone while running toward the crash.
  - **Latina witness:** Calls her psychic on her cell phone while running back into the house.

- **Anglo witness:** Searches for the victims' wallets to identify them.
- **Latino witness:** Searches for the victims' wallets to identify them. What did you think I was going to say?
- **Anglo witness:** Instructs the other witnesses not to move the injured until the paramedics arrive.
- **Latino witness:** Instructs other witnesses to pull out a strand of hair from each of the injured, tie them all together, and wrap it around a white candle.

- *Situation D.* Your brother rushes into your house, injured. His whole right arm is badly scraped up. How do you handle the situation?
  - **Anglo sibling:** Grabs the keys and drives him to the nearest emergency room.
  - **Latino sibling:** Grabs the keys and rubs them over the affected area. It's a family remedy.
  - **Anglo sibling:** Gets some ice and towels to deal with the inflammation.
  - **Latino sibling:** Gets some ice and scotch to deal with the sight of blood.
  - **Anglo sibling:** Gives him two painkillers to get through the night. Tomorrow he'll feel better.
  - **Latino sibling:** Gives him one of Grandma's home-made potions to get through the night. Tomorrow he'll throw up all day while insisting he is a jaguar.

- *Situation E.* Your flight is delayed, and you have to wait at least two more hours until another plane arrives. What do you do?
  - **Anglo passenger:** Makes a note of the flight number and the gate, then leaves to buy himself a nice dinner, because there's no reason to sit there doing nothing.

- **Latino passenger:** Makes a note of the flight number and the gate, then leaves to buy a lotto ticket with those numbers, because there's always a reason behind everything.
- **Anglo passenger:** Tells the man next to him: "I hope we board before midnight."
- **Latino passenger:** Tells the man next to him: "We've got a pool going on whether we board before midnight, you want in for ten bucks?"
- **Anglo passenger:** Goes to the kiosk, buys the *Wall Street Journal*, and enjoys some good reading.
- **Latina passenger:** Goes to her luggage, pulls out a bunch of tabloids and magazines and starts reading them out loud and crying at the same time. She's learning what's going on with the stars of her favorite *novelas*.

CHAPTER 25

Latino Folk Illnesses

If you've ever felt that there was something wrong with you, but no doctor would confirm it, you might find what you're looking for here. We'll begin our journey with three of the most common Latino folk illnesses, as well as the remarkable rituals and ceremonies the *curanderos* throughout Latin America perform to treat them. The information in this chapter can save your life, but not because it's going to diagnose what's actually wrong with you in any way. What it will do is help you interpret your *curandero's* diagnosis in a more informed manner.

Latino Folk Illness #1: *"Mal de Ojo"* (Evil Eye)
This belief is based on the principle that some people, driven by envy of other people's luck or good looks, can curse them just by staring while thinking: *"Why you? Why not me? You don't deserve that! I hate you! I hope you die by fire!"* Basically, the average Hollywood casting call.

This malady is very basic to cure, sort of a *curanderos* 101. Even my grandmother could diagnose and remedy it. The curse begins with a tremendous headache, but some cultures believe the evil eye can cause disease or even death. The *curandero* whispers a secret prayer and makes the sign of the cross repeatedly with his thumb on your forehead. The prayer has to be repeated three times. I always tried to hear the prayer, to steal the secret power from my grandma. I guess she could tell, because she told me that only *curanderos* could learn it. I asked, "Are you a *curandera*, Grandma?" "No," she replied. That didn't make any sense, but I was nine at the time, and fooling me was easy.

Later, she explained that the prayer has to be revealed only under special circumstances—such as on a *curandero*'s deathbed, on Christmas Eve at midnight, the moment before he expires. That's how hard it is to get. You either have to be very lucky with the timing or else use poison, I guess.

Every time I had a headache, she was happy to get some practice on the evil eye. "*Estás ojeado, m'hijito!*" (You've been busted, son!) She would cross me and recite the secret prayer, and when the headache persisted, she'd repeat it again and again. According to tradition, if one is indeed afflicted with the evil eye, both victim and healer start to yawn excessively during the ritual. For a boy my age, this process was as dull as sitting in church, and my grandmother was eighty-two, so I can attest to a great deal of yawning. There's your proof, nonbelievers.

Although you'll always need a *curandero* to get rid of the evil eye, there's a simple way to protect yourself from getting the affliction in the first place. You should always wear something red—a shirt, underwear, or even a red string on your wrist. That's it—that's all you need. The bad spirits do wrong 24/7, but you won't be affected, or so they say. The one exception is if you travel to Pamplona, Spain, during the running of the bulls. You'd rather have the evil eye than the pierced butt.

PUTTING YOUR NEW KNOWLEDGE TO USE.

Imagine yourself arriving at the office one morning just in time to hear your Latino colleague complaining about a headache. Don't just blurt out, "Pedro, you have the evil eye!" Instead of thanking you for your thoughtfulness, Pedro may suspect you of being the cause of his headache, and he may start asking himself questions: Why is this Anglo sharing my curses with everyone? Why does he know so much about evil eye? You don't want to trade an evil eye for a black one, so try a friendly, "Do you have a minute, Pedro?" Before you know it, you might have a little side business running out of your cubicle.

Latino Folk Illness #2: *"Empacho"* (Surfeit)
It means "impacted stomach," and it's related to some kind of indigestion due to the adherence of food to the stomach wall. It is most common in young children, and the major symptoms are stomachache and a feeling of abdominal fullness.

If you are an Anglo kid, your parents give you Tums or Pepto-Bismol. When you are a Latino child and your stomach hurts, telling your parents is the last resort. You really have to be suffering. Then you get to the point where you feel like you are dying. But you still don't say a word—seriously, until you see blood somewhere. This is because the remedy is worse than the disease; I call it Latino preventative medicine. If you don't clean your plate at dinner, they call the *curandero*. There are a lot of ways to diagnose the illness. One way is to roll an egg over the patient's abdomen. If the egg sticks to a certain area, *empacho* is confirmed.

"So, your parents tell me you did not finish dinner?"

"I ate four Popsicles before I came in, it was so hot today."

"Don't get smart, can't you see the egg sticks to your stomach!"

"So did some lint, a baseball card, and a Popsicle stick; I'm a messy eater."

"Don't argue."

The treatment varies depending on the country, so I'll tell you what my own grandma used to do. Her remedy was pulling the skin on my back, and snapping it like a rubber band. It would start pleasantly enough: She would rub a powder of some kind on my back. It'd feel nice, but then she'd grab a piece of skin and she'd pull it up and thwwwwack! I'd scream, but nobody would sympathize. She'd keep going, looking for the right spot, the one that was going to heal me. Apparently, her "natural ability" to heal gave her no clue about what part of the back held the key to the cure, so she kept thwacking my skin until she heard the right sound. According to her, there was air trapped under the skin, and that's the cause of the *empacho*. Once the air is released, the patient is cured. It doesn't matter how long or painful the process. Instead of calling the cops after hearing an eight-year-old scream for an hour, the neighbors all nod in agreement, "He's *empachado* again."

Now, let's keep this knowledge in perspective. If tomorrow on the street you see a Latino girl pinning down another girl and pulling the skin of her back, please don't assume, "Oh, I read about this! A *curandera* helping with *empacho*." This is not something we do in the middle of the day in front of everybody. There's no healing going on there—they're probably two sisters fighting over a boyfriend. Don't worry, though, they will go see their *curandera* as soon as the police release them.

Latino Folk Illness #3: *"Susto"* (Fright)
Did you ever hear the phrase "I was so scared my heart jumped out of my body"? This folk illness is based on the same principle,

but it's the soul that flees. It's caused by a sudden frightening experience, such as an accident, a fall, witnessing a death, or any other dangerous or shocking event. For example, when you are an illegal immigrant, and *la migra* is around the neighborhood, you panic, your heart beats faster than ever, the adrenaline level goes sky high, and you think you'll have a heart attack if they find you. Hours later, you crawl out of bed and they're gone, but you can feel that something's still wrong. You conclude that your soul has fled your body, and it's not coming back . . . unless you find a good *curandero*.

Unfortunately, my grandma didn't know how to treat somebody suffering from *susto* (unfortunately for you, that is, but lucky for me) so I had to do some research. From what I've found, the most accepted treatment for *susto* is a ceremony known as the *barrida*, or sweeping. During the *barrida*, the patient recounts the details of the frightening event then lies down on the floor. The patient's body is then swept with fresh herbs; an egg may also be used (they can diagnose your *empacho* at the same time!). During the sweeping, the *curandero* and other participants say ritual prayers, exhorting the frightened soul to return to the body. In some countries, the *curandero* may also jump over the patient's body during the ceremony. I personally think that since a *curandero* cannot laugh at you in your face for letting him rip you off your money, this is the way he uses to tell you, "You are so dumb I can even jump on your limbs and get away with it."

Overall, I think this is the most foolproof diagnosis. With physical conditions like a headache, either the pain goes away and you have cured them (or you are extremely lucky) or it doesn't, and they will voice the news all over the barrio and you won't be a *curandero* anymore.

To sum this issue up, I propose that if in order to blend in with the rest of U.S. society we have to sacrifice some customs, we should start with our folk illnesses. Every culture had its dark ages, its quirky home remedies, and its nonsensical ailments— the trick we seem to have missed is to put them on the shelf as curiosities, have a good laugh about them, and for heaven's sake leave your grandson's back alone.

CHAPTER 26

THE LATINO RESTAURANT

There are things that are deserved and other things that just happen, but fate always warns us by means of an "intuition." When you accept your friends' invitation to go out for dinner next weekend, and all of a sudden you feel a stomach pain, what's that if not a sign? It could be gas. These friends, all of them Anglo, are the kind of people who like to get a taste of adventure, to go after different experiences. They get bored easily and think a parachute jump sounds fun. They're always trying out new things, as if life were made to enjoy.

Their plan for this weekend: to have dinner in a recently opened Latino restaurant, whose renowned chef has worked in every five-star hotel kitchen throughout Latin America. Located near a residential villa, the prices indicate refined food and impeccable service. The day before the gathering, you have the bad luck of losing a porcelain crown from the right side of your mouth. You suppose it is a coincidence, yet it's nothing short of another sign.

Saturday night arrives, and everybody meets up at the restaurant. The building looks expensive, the type of restaurant that would earn a "5 forks" review. There is a big sign over the door that reads *"La Cocina de la Abuela"* (Grandma's Kitchen) with the tagline "Specialists in Latin American Dishes." The sign suggests all the dishes are made of natural ingredients prepared with the same love and dedication a grandma has for her family. Never mind that your own grandma used to burn boiled eggs, undercook instant rice, and even chop lettuce in a way that somehow made it taste worse. Even delivery food tasted bad when she ordered it. Your grandfather didn't die of old age, he starved himself. Yet another sign.

There's also a more significant piece of information: the tagline "Specialists in Latin American Dishes." As we've covered throughout the book, Latin America is not a single place, but a wide group of countries, each one of them with its own culture, customs, and in many cases totally different gastronomic influences. To say "Latin American Dishes" is as vague as to say "fish" when someone is referring to marine life.

All of these little things combined start to sow some doubt in your mind. You push this feeling aside when your friends say they have been dying to try out this restaurant after seeing a full-page ad in *Eating Today* magazine. You joke nervously that you'd feel more comfortable if the magazine were called *Eating Tomorrow*. Your friends don't laugh.

Once seated, you discover that the menu is written in Spanish, and the waiter speaks no English. The evening's organizer decides to order on behalf of everybody, since he did spend some time with a Spanish-language CD-ROM he picked up at the Price Club. The food comes, and just by looking at it, you know you don't want to eat it. What excuse would be good enough to run away, leaving your friends behind? Your only shot is to wait for them to start eating before you do, and if anybody drops dead, it'd be a good reason to leave the plate untouched. But nothing happens; they eat and chat, enjoying their meal. At some point, somebody says to you: "Are you going to eat or what? It's getting cold!" You weren't even sure if you'd been served a hot or cold dish. You close your eyes, take a deep breath, and swallow. It's delicious! A perfect mix of different flavors, not too spicy, not too sweet; the "Latin American dish" comes together smoothly. You've overcome your fears and can enjoy the meal; the signs were wrong.

By the time the main course arrives at the table, you're starting to think of yourself as a Latin American citizen. You feel like you have traveled throughout the continent tasting unforgettable indigenous flavors. Without hesitation, you plunge your fork into the new dish. It's different. It is, you might say, nasty. If it's meat, it's so musty it could be wooly mammoth, and it's also overspiced to mask the rotten flavor. By that time, your adventurous friends have imbibed glasses, buckets, and ponds of margaritas. As the designated driver, you're the only one sober enough to discern the dish is not good. Later, the waiter takes your plate and asks, "Everything okay, sir? You didn't touch your food. Did you like it?" When you casually answer "no," you start a series of unfortunate events beyond your wildest imaginings. The waiter replies he'll let the chef know about it, so he can replace it with something else.

FEAR SAYS HELLO!

The chef already knows you didn't like your meal, because the waiter tipped him off. You fear that passing on dessert is not an option, because it'll be pushing the issue too far. The chef could decide to step out of the kitchen to pay a visit to your table, and nobody wants that. Well, to be honest, your friends are too wasted to care.

Question: What body part will the angry chef dip in your dessert?

Answer: All that fit, so order something blazing hot or freezing cold.

When your dessert arrives, it appears the chef has taken certain artistic license in his interpretation of molten chocolate lava cake. His version is in fact a pumpkin with a knife stuck in it and a note that says "You."

Latinos take everything personally. We're not able to differentiate between what we do and what we are. If you don't like the food, a Latino chef hears that you think he can't cook. Ty Cobb, baseball's all-time batting average leader, hit an astounding .367, which still means he missed more than he hit. It's a real shame you won't have time to explain this delightful analogy to the chef of "Grandma's Kitchen" as you run screaming out of the restaurant.

CHAPTER 27

How to Know If Your Girlfriend Is Latina . . .

At this point, you have acquired a lot of knowledge about Latinas. You know how they look. You know what they love. You know how to treat them. However, identifying one of them among other females can be tricky sometimes.

As incredible as it may seem, not every Latino last name sounds like González or García. On the other hand, not every Rosa is Latina.

Reluctant to deal with inequality and discrimination, some Latinos opt to hide their Hispanic heritage. I'm not just talking about third-generation Latinos. I mean the immigrants who might not have arrived in this country so long ago, but they're able to speak proper English and otherwise blend in.

You could ask yourself: "If they don't look Latino, don't talk like a Latino, and don't have Latino habits, who cares if they're Latino or not?" Believe me; you should care, a lot. The Latino soul and spirit are always there, latent, ready to manifest when you least expect it. In your girlfriend's case, she herself might not even know what she is; perhaps she lost her memory in a car accident three years ago. How can you be completely sure?

Check out the following list:

1. Show up at her house, unexpectedly.
   Non-Latina girlfriend: She's watching *CSI: New York*.
   Latina girlfriend: She's watching a *telenovela* in Spanish called *My Hundred Children*.

2. Bring her with you to the paint store.
   Non-Latina girlfriend: Suggests some color palettes.
   Latina girlfriend: Grabs five gallons of orange for the walls, one of green for the doors, and a small can of silver to spray the chairs, without ever asking your opinion.

3. Hide in a closet, and as soon as your girlfriend walks in the room, jump out screaming to scare the hell out of her.
   Non-Latina girlfriend: She passes out.
   Latina girlfriend: She yells, "*Ay, carajo!*" and starts chasing you to kick you in the groin.

4. Come home before her to check the answering machine.
   Non-Latina girlfriend: "You have no new messages."
   Latina girlfriend: "You have 522 messages." The first eight are from "Uncle Jose."

5. Play a Gloria Estefan song, in Spanish.
   Non-Latina girlfriend: She says, "I think she sounds better in English."

Latina girlfriend: She starts singing along and dancing frantically.

6. Play "Born in the U.S.A." by Bruce Springsteen.
   Non-Latina girlfriend: She starts singing along.
   Latina girlfriend: She starts singing along, but in Spanish.

7. Go out on a date and take her to a dessert-only restaurant.
   Non-Latina girlfriend: Says, "I'll just have a decaf."
   Latina girlfriend: Somehow spends more than if you'd had dinner.

8. Invite her on a vacation tour throughout Latin America.
   Non-Latina girlfriend: She buys an English-Spanish dictionary before the trip.
   Latina girlfriend: She comes back to the States with twelve members of her family she didn't know she had.

CHAPTER 28

Lost in a Latino Neighborhood . . .

Before we begin, there are some things you ought to know about Latino neighborhoods. The key is not what to do but what *not* to do. Please read, memorize, and apply the following list any time you go out on a trip that involves passing by *a 'hood*.

TOP FIVE THINGS TO AVOID IN A LATINO NEIGHBORHOOD:

5. Buying food on the streets.

   You may be an ex–Green Beret who is now in a motor-cycle gang, very tough on the outside. But unless you have been training your insides just as rigorously, they are soft and pink and unfit to tame Latin street food. A Latino child's guts have not only been to boot camp, they are like the drill sergeant that never left.

4. Calling the police.

   You won't get past 9-1 . . . Nobody wants the police there—not even the grandmothers, who will slap the phone right out of your hand.

3. Picking things up off the street.
   While you shouldn't do this in any neighborhood, in a Latino neighborhood it's probably an amulet left there as part of a curse. If you already touched it, run away yelling, "The power of Christ compels you! The power of Christ compels you!"

2. Making eye contact with a woman.
   Do you have any idea whether this woman is involved? Me neither, but don't be naïve. In a Latino neighborhood, there's not one unclaimed woman over thirteen years old.

1. Going to a party.
   Are you crazy? Even if they invited you and called it a "barbecue," it's going to be ten armed men, no chips, and calling your family for a ransom.

I always wondered why Anglos are so afraid of Latino neighborhoods. I think it's because of the movies. Every action movie and thriller has a main character, a brave and fearless male, who desperately searches for his best friend's murderer by speeding over sidewalks and median strips in a wrecked car. A dirty trick of destiny causes his ride to break down in the middle of a Latino neighborhood: poorly lit streets, garbage all around, decrepit buildings, homeless people sleeping on benches, and a gang assaulting an old lady on the corner.

I categorically deny this representation of a Latino neighborhood. In reality, they're not nearly so poorly lit. And as an actor, I can't help having a bunch of rewrites for the script, so let's start by putting you in the picture. Let's say you're the star of the movie, but you're not looking for your friend's murderer, you're just lost.

Let's assume it's noon, the buildings are in regular condition, and there are no homeless around—we'll keep the gang assaulting the old lady, for the sake of realism. Your cell phone has died and there are no pay phones around. Actually, there are many, but they look unsanitary. You survey the situation and decide the best thing to do is to knock on a stranger's door and ask for help. You will encounter a variety of archetypes. Let's analyze the most common:

HOUSE #1—THE ILLEGALS.

There are four cars parked in the driveway. One of them is missing the tires, the seats, and the windows and might be better described as a "planter box," but let's call it a car anyway. As you walk toward the front door, you catch a glimpse of eyes peering at you through a curtain. Oddly, nobody answers the doorbell. Not only are there people in the house, but you can hear them all scrambling around. You glimpse through the window and see a bunch of arms and legs sticking out from beneath the sofa. Now everything is clear; the tenants are illegal immigrants, and they've mistaken you for an Immigration officer. Your first impulse is to yell, "Open the door, I'm not from Immigration!" But something stops you: you sense that this mistaken identity might be what's keeping you unharmed in the neighborhood.

HOUSE #2—THE READING.

You knock on a door, and it opens promptly. A Latina who looks like she's ninety-five years old opens the door. First thing she does, she calls her mother. Another lady shows up (she looks a hundred and fifteen) and she exclaims, *"Un cliente!"* You try to protest, but you are dragged to the small dark living room, crammed full of aromatic candles and skeleton bones. She tells you to sit down and listen. During the next two hours, you nod at every word that comes out of the woman's mouth as she tells you that you are going to be robbed, you will marry, and you are going to be happy. Those are the only things you can understand, since she speaks little English. When she sends you on your way, she charges you a hundred bucks. This bodes well for your future, because already her predictions are coming true.

HOUSE #3—THE MESSENGER.

As you walk up the steps to this house, the door flies open and a man emerges. He's a little over five feet tall, with a black mustache. He shoves a wrapped package in your hands and says: "Johnny wants this next to the other deliveries, same price."

You barely have the package between your hands when the door is closed again. Trembling, you knock on the door. You tell the little man, "Johnny changed the plans, he wants double or nothing, call him up." He surely will decide to double-check the information before killing you, so he takes the package, saying he's going to phone Johnny. Sensing this is your last chance, you run back to the street, but your car is not there anymore. You'd rather do anything than spend another minute in this insane asylum of a neighborhood, so you start running back toward civilization.

An hour later, still jogging down the road and sweaty to the bone, you are passed by a car resembling yours down to the last detail. In the passenger seat is the old lady who was being assaulted, and she's accompanied by the gang members, one of whom is driving, the psychic and her daughter, and a number of the illegal aliens who had been hiding under the couch. She's opening the package Johnny ordered, and at that moment, you realize that this wasn't a neighborhood of criminals—they were a big family celebrating Grandma's one hundredth birthday!

CHAPTER 29

WHAT HAPPENS WHEN YOUR CHILD'S TEACHER IS LATINA ...

I'm sure when you went to school your teachers were U.S.-born, with the same culture, customs, and history as you. Welcome to the twenty-first century, where globalization, diversification, and the equal job opportunity laws make it possible—even very likely—for your child's school to employ foreign-born teachers.

BACK TO SCHOOL.

Your son, little Kevin, just turned six years old. You drop him off for his first day, and everything is fresh and exciting: he's wearing his brand-new uniform, superhero backpack, combed hair, and smelling like soap. This year Kevin will learn how to write and read. He'll learn about his country's history and the meaning of patriotism. On his classroom door, there's a handwritten sign that says: "Ms. Gonzalez." You quickly learn that Ms. Gonzalez arrived from Mexico eight years ago, she's forty, and word is she's an excellent teacher. You tell yourself that's all that should matter.

A Latina teacher introduces some funny paradoxes, like having a Mexican teach U.S. history to a local. Not that there's anything wrong with that, but if you were about to hire a midwife, would you consider a man? We always want an instructor with firsthand experience by our side, regardless of the activity. If you're going to take a physics course, you'd love to have Einstein as a teacher. If you're going to play baseball, you want to be by Derek Jeter's side. A Latina teacher can have mastered her skills at a higher level than an American, but our brains are still wired so that we feel more comfortable with someone of similar background.

For these reasons, you were a bit worried for your little Kevin. You were even more concerned when, one evening, Kevin said, *"Hasta mañana"* instead of "Good night." A month later, you heard him say, "I can't stand these gringos," and you panicked. Were you justified? Let's review the situation in a calm, rational way.

YOUR CHILD'S LATINA TEACHER IS DOING A POOR JOB WHEN:

1. She teaches her own version of American history.
    *   **JFK assassination:** One day, the president wanted to go for a ride in his hydraulic lowrider convertible. On the road, he crossed into a rival gang's territory—the Texas Oil Kings. They busted a cap in his dome, and like Teflon dons, they pinned the rap on a patsy.
    *   **Landing on the moon:** In an attempt to illegally cross the U.S. border, a Mexican named Lil' Frog strapped four rocket engines to his 1957 Chevrolet Bel Air hardtop. In eight minutes, his vehicle went from zero to 17,000 mph, hit a rock, and left Earth's gravitational pull. When he landed on the moon, he thought it was San Diego, and to fit in better, he stuck a U.S. flag in the ground next to him. NASA has never been able to duplicate Lil' Frog's achievement, so instead

they made a moon-landing movie with some very fake-looking special effects.

- **Bill Clinton's affair:** In a noble gesture, the president invited one of his White House interns to tour the Oval Office. She gladly accepted, and right in the middle of her visit, she noticed his fly was open. She whispered this information to him, and when he looked down to zip his pants, the president lost a contact lens. As she fell to her knees to pray to Santa Lucía, patron saint of eyes and blindness, the president, unable to see out of one eye and having no depth perception, stepped forward, getting his zipper caught in her retainer. At this exact moment, Kenneth Starr walked in and misunderstood everything. This happens to everyone at one time or another; how do you think I got this job?

- **Independence Day:** Whether you want to be independent of poverty, your mother-in-law, or a home-wrecking mistress, July 4 is the day Americans set aside to make it happen. They use firecrackers, bottle rockets, and roman candles to make so much noise that if you shoot someone, set a building on fire, or even rob a liquor store, the police won't know until the morning.

2. She makes up holidays and claims they are "cultural education."
   - **National Salsa Day:** All the little children learn to shake their hips like crazy, then early dismissal.
   - **Anniversary of Fidel Castro's Death:** Since he is still alive, she picks a day at random and celebrates with early dismissal and a fine cigar.
   - **Illegal Immigrants Day:** Any child who can sneak

past the crossing guard gets early dismissal, but once home, they have to do twice the schoolwork for half the credit.

3. Her PTA is a P.I.T.A.

Ms. Gonzalez specifies a 4:30 p.m. start time, so all the parents are forced to take a half day at work or beg to leave early. All of the Anglo parents are there by 4:15, but the father of the only Latino student in the school, Ramon Galvez, doesn't arrive until 5:08 p.m. Ms. Gonzalez herself also arrives at 5:08, as if they are both privy to a conversion chart.

First thing, Ms. Gonzalez asks if everybody there speaks English. Mr. Galvez raises his hand and says "no." Fifty years ago, the other seventy parents in the room would have agreed that it's his responsibility to learn it, but the world has changed. Nobody complains when Ms. Gonzalez announces she's going to give her talk in both languages. What was going to last ninety minutes will now last three hours.

4. She openly tells the students what gifts she wants for teacher's day.

She doesn't want a card or an apple. At the beginning of the year, she distributes the student supply list, including a separate page entitled: "Your *maestra* wishes..." That list includes eyeliner, Spanish-language magazines, bath foam, potting soil, glass cleaner, cornmeal, nylons, aspirin, mud mask, stain remover spray, hand lotion, 75-watt lightbulbs, bird seed, deep treatment hair conditioner, adhesive bandages, bug spray, powdered sugar, cotton balls, and so on.

5. She asks for a private meeting with some of the students' fathers before handing out grades.

- She urgently needs to meet with two categories of fathers: the wealthiest and the best-looking. They must meet privately to discuss educational issues . . . at her house . . . at night . . . on a Saturday. This is appropriate, because she is both single and curvaceous.
- If the father doesn't show up, his child gets an F, as in "F you, too."
- If the father shows up with his wife, their child gets a D, as in "Dummy, catch a clue!"
- If the father shows up by himself, well groomed and smelling like cologne, his child gets an A, as in "*¡Ay, papi!*"

If your children's teacher is Latina, you have to be extra sure you teach them your own U.S. values. Children absorb teachings from grown-ups as absolute truths, and the last thing you need is for your kids to start quoting Che Guevara and making plans to join up with their freedom-fighting "brothers" in some jungle.

CHAPTER 30

So Your Neighbor Is a "New Rich" Latino . . . (Rules of Coexistence)

Not so long ago, some barriers seemed impenetrable. There were places where Anglos could expect to be around people like themselves, and no one else. Today, there is no wall high enough to keep out the changes of modern society. Money rules, and "a million is a million," regardless of who possesses it. Old-money families who thought they were never going to have Latino neighbors were wrong. Thanks to the many blessings of the land of opportunity, twenty-first-century Latinos can afford houses in exclusive neighborhoods, fenced and guarded by men who in previous eras were hired to keep people like them out. In addition, Latinos can sometimes even achieve this money through *legal* activities.

COMMUNITY STANDARDS.

The house next door to yours had been on sale for a couple of months. You were surprised one day to see the sold sign, since it seemed so overpriced. From that moment, the rumors about the new neighbors within the community started running. Did a doctor buy the house, or a politician, or maybe even a famous actor or athlete?

The previous year, you had attended the annual home owners' meeting for the neighborhood. Someone suggested a committee to evaluate and approve prospective home buyers in the exclusive community. The prevailing opinion was magnanimous and democratic: "Whoever is loaded enough to afford these prices is welcome in the neighborhood." Folks who don't read the papers, it's time to wake up and smell the coffee! Nowadays, anybody can become a millionaire. Wealth doesn't guarantee education, morals, or class whatsoever—to be honest, it never did.

Checking on the county Web site, you discover the new owner's last name: Vazqueño. The n with the tilde over it? That character is not present in the English language: your new neighbors are Latino.

THE MOVE-iN.

It's six thirty a.m. on Saturday morning. Three black eighteen-wheelers park in front of the house next door, taking up half the block. Gazing from your bathroom window, you see an impressive sight: twenty-five men running back and forth from the trucks, unloading furniture and hundreds of boxes. The yelling is so loud it sounds like they are right there in the Jacuzzi with you. Then you realize the yelling doesn't come from the movers, who are precise, efficient, and use walkie-talkies rather than shouting. The racket is coming from a party. Thirty-two people are playing baseball and barbecuing ribs in the front yard—where just ten minutes ago there was nothing louder than green grass and geraniums.

You try to sympathize: new house, new neighborhood . . . they must feel like fish out of water, so they decided to celebrate among friends. But this is a misunderstanding on your part, because all thirty-two of the people trampling the lawns and flower beds of that house (as well as yours) are members of the Vazqueño family. By five p.m., the move-in is finished. The noise, on the other hand, is here to stay.

WELCOME TO THE NEIGHBORHOOD.
Setting your reservations aside, you acknowledge that a good neighbor is defined by his friendliness. You pay a visit to the Vazqueño house, carrying a housewarming gift—a leather pen cup. When you buy a gift, you should do it thinking of the recipient, so it fits them. You haven't even been introduced to your neighbor—you have a point there. But you know it's a Latino family—I have a point here. That sole piece of information should be enough to steer you in the right direction. For example:

- A framed embroidery reading *Hogar Dulce Hogar* (Home Sweet Home) and a bottle of tequila.
- An Aztec warrior virgin sacrifice poster, and a bottle of tequila.
- A *No Cerveza, No Trabajo* (no beer, no work) baseball cap and a bottle of tequila.
- A velvet painting of a sad clown and a bottle of tequila.
- Two bottles of tequila.

SPIES LIKE US.
After presenting your gift, you'll probably be invited inside and given a tour of the house. Avoid letting your jaw drop or eyes bug out. I don't want to frighten you, but the last thing you want is a Latino head of household thinking, "This gringo disapproves of

my castle?!" The dining room curtains are purple, yes. It's the color of royalty, in case you didn't know. There's so much furniture in the living room it looks like a retail showroom. There are so many mirrors you half expect to turn the corner and find Bruce Lee fighting his archnemesis, Han.

BOUNDARY ISSUES.

Your attempt at neighborly civility will convince Mr. Vazqueño that you would like to be best friends. Latinos are friendly by nature, and in most cases a little too friendly. He'll soon consider you his *pana* and *chamo* (his brother and compadre). He considers himself your friend, your wife's friend, and your kids' friend. He believes he's a friend of your friends, of your wife's friends, of your children's friends, and even of your children's friends' parents.

He'll invite you over for dinner with his family, he'll expect you to invite him over for dinner with your family, and he'll also expect your children's friends' parents to invite him over. It's time to start thinking of excuses, nothing too rude. It's not your intention to hurt his feelings, but to let him know as politely as possible that all you're looking for is the occasional hand wave over the fence.

Here are a number of suitable excuses with a range in rudeness, as required:

- **Mild:** "My wife's agoraphobic and she barely goes out. Thank you for understanding, and we'll see if her condition is improved next year."
- **Medium:** "We were close friends with the previous owners of your house, and they died in a horrible accident. You don't think superstition is silly, do you?"

- **Hot:** "We voted against bilingual education in schools, and we hope you will, too. Learn English, amiright?"
- **Jalapeño Hot:** "I can't wait to introduce your whole family to my brother. He has a big head now that he's high level with the INS, but I'll always think of him as my little shadow."

FROM RESISTANCE TO COEXISTENCE.

You regret not having bought a bigger piece of land, not because you love the outdoors, but at least if you were farther away you could avoid the smell of Latino food that seeps into your living room. Not to mention the grease sticking to your windows, making them look like submarine portholes. Your wife doesn't like it that Vazqueño's wife sunbathes naked in their backyard. On the

Here I am at a karaoke party in my house. It's six a.m., and I'm singing out loud (and out of tune). We are on the terrace. I'm surrounded by Anglo neighbors. Now that I see the picture, I understand why they called the cops.

153

one hand, it is their property. On the other, climbing the fifteen-foot-high ladder to dive into the pool nude is a bit out of line when the fences are five feet high.

Having your neighbors outside all weekend long—yelling, smoking like chimneys, and tearing oranges from the tree on your property—you can live with. Throwing the cigarette butts and orange peels over the fence to your side is too much. Still looking for answers? Still begging for a solution? There's only one thing you can do: if you can't beat them, join them. It might be easier than you think, which brings us to our next chapter.

CHAPTER 31

Surprise, You're a Latino Yourself!

What would happen if you found out you weren't who you thought you were? What factors play a role in determining the way people are? Is it all about the genes, or is it the specific circumstances in which we were raised? Personally, I like to believe it's a mix of both factors. I could be genetically gifted to be a lion tamer, but if my father doesn't happen to work in a circus, I'd never even find out about my gift. I don't want to elaborate on existential theories, but I wonder what would happen if some genetic factor were discovered in midlife. If the gifted lion tamer doesn't see his first big cat until age fifty-two, should he still honor his gift? Should he leave his Chicago-based law firm to tour around the world with the bearded lady and JoJo the Dog-faced Boy? If at age forty an Anglo finds out his father's "real" last name was Lopez, will it change his behavior? I don't know, but at least it explains why he had the jitters telling Canadian customs he didn't have any fruit in the car.

Let's explore how this kind of story could begin. Ronald Hughes, forty-one years old, was born in Milwaukee. At eighteen, he headed to college, and three years later he dropped out to be a cell phone salesman in Manhattan. One day, his father, Greg Hughes, passes away. Ronald goes back to Milwaukee for the funeral. The rest of the family welcomes Ronald with the usual clichés: "It was a surprise for everybody," "He was so good," and "It was a tragedy."

After the burial service, the family's attorney specifies that there is a will, and it should be read before any visiting family members fly back home. Everybody gathers in the dining room. The lawyer sits at the head of the table, double-checking the document, while Ronald, his mother, siblings, uncles, aunts, and cousins wait expectantly.

The attorney starts by reading: "I, Greg Hughes *Lopez*, hereby bequeath . . ." The next events are right out of the movies: The scene slows down like someone fired a bunch of bullets at Neo in *The Matrix*, then fear sweeps the room like the beach in *Jaws*, then a total pandemonium of knocking over lamps and catching the drapes on fire, like a scene from *Meet the Parents*. Ronald jumps out of his chair and grabs the attorney by his neck, demanding an explanation. There is no mistake. Greg took his secret to his grave, but it is revealed while his body is still warm: He had been born in Colombia and his own father's last name was Lopez. At this point, some pieces of the family puzzle begin to fall into place. For example, Greg's childhood photos on a coffee plantation, of which there are none in Milwaukee . . . not to mention his ability to make the best espresso-macchiato in the state of Wisconsin. His last bequest wasn't money; there was none. It was the gift of an endlessly rich cultural heritage.

THE NEW ME.

Ronald goes out to the backyard, trying to pull himself together. He feels like the monster from the film *Alien* is tearing his body apart from the inside out, though this movie would have to be called *Illegal Alien*. At first sight, it seems foolish, because nothing has really changed for him. He can continue to lead his life as he has for forty years. But at the same time, knowing his veins are half full of Latino blood is the biggest revelation of his life. To evolve or die, that's the question.

Ronald sets off on a walk, absorbed in his thoughts. While he is crossing the street without looking, a car almost hits him. He rummages through his pockets for gum, pops a piece into his mouth, and drops the wrapper on the street. A policeman gives him a ticket for littering. Ronald has been Latino for thirty minutes, and already he hates gringos.

Saying "*Hasta la vista, baby*" to the rest of the family, "Ronaldo" takes a bus back to New York. Over the course of the ride, his mind goes through what the psychiatrist Elisabeth Kübler-Ross calls the five stages of grief:

1. Denial.
   I can't be Latino. I failed Spanish, think Penélope Cruz is overrated, and don't care about soap operas.

2. Anger.
   Why did my father never tell me about his true origins? Because he's a goddamn shifty Latino, that's why!

3. Bargaining.
   I can go to the New York Blood Center and get a complete transfusion. But with my luck I'll go from half Latino to full-blooded Chinese and be even more confused.

4. Depression.
   I don't belong here, nor there. I'm not from another country; I'm from another planet.

5. Acceptance.

What the hell am I saying? I have the best of both worlds! I'm a first-class citizen and also a macho Latin lover. I can cross the border freely and also dance the salsa. I can go to SoHo and buy the brightest colored clothes, then put them on all at once, even for a loan interview or funeral.

GETTING BACK TO NORMAL.

Ronald arrives in the Big Apple. He greets strangers by saying "*Hola*" and buys two bootlegged Gloria Estefan CDs in Times Square. Ronald Hughes Lopez feels Latino, and he likes it. He wants to greet women with a kiss, forget his English, and evade taxes. He decides to trace his father's footsteps back all the way to Colombia. He makes some calls, does some research on the Internet, and discovers what I call his "Latino inheritance":

• He has seven half brothers and twelve cousins living in Colombia, some of them in Bogotá and the rest in Medellín.
• His father had a debt in that country, which his son is expected to honor.
• As soon as they found out about his existence, four of his half brothers sent him letters asking for loans (the other three are illiterate).
• He receives four marriage proposals—three from transsexuals, and the fourth from a prostitute.

Ronald understands that he is opening a Pandora's box, but he feels compelled. There's nothing he can do about it. He asks himself: "What do I need to do in order to be a real U.S. Latino?"

He talks to all the Latinos he can find and he writes down a list. Here you have a transcription of that list.

THE TEN MOST IMPORTANT THINGS TO DO TO BECOME A REAL U.S. LATINO:

10. Learn Spanish, but mix it with English.

9. Talk about your Latino country with love and passion, even if you've never been there.

8. Call a cousin in the old country and brag about how much money you are making.

7. Remove the landscaping from your front yard to make space for the barbecue pit.

6. Tell the story of how your immigrant father immigrated, struggled to become a citizen, and worked triple shifts to pay for your education. If you don't have that kind of story, make one up.

5. Have a couple of anecdotes about being discriminated against at school, work, or when crossing a border. If you have none of those, make them up!

4. Watch your *novelas* every day.

3. Choose a saint, buy a life-sized statue of him, and start asking for favors, performing rituals, and promising sacrifices.

2. Start eating all the Latino dishes, including the tripe and tongue you've been avoiding.

1. Get yourself a Latina girlfriend.

He decides the first order of business is to find a Latina girlfriend. He calls up Antonia, his undocumented cleaning lady. The old Ronald saw her as cheap labor and an opportunity to sell a $780 phone she neither needed nor could afford. The new Ronaldo sees a completely different woman, a human being cut from the same cloth, looking for the same things, with the same background and struggles. He asks Antonia out, they get to know each other, and they fall deeply in love. They move in together right away, then after a year, they get married.

As the years go by, Antonia can't believe she once saw Ronald as a greedy, heartless gringo. Now he is so completely different— a typical Latino husband who makes her cook, mop, iron, take care of the children, never talk to another man, never have any money of her own, and never dress sexy, even as he ogles every woman in the neighborhood.

If Grandpa Lopez could just see him now . . . he'd be so proud of "Ronaldo"!

CHAPTER 32

TEST #2—PARA BAILAR LA BAMBA

As we reach the end of another part of our journey, I'm obliged to test your Latino-ness once again. Don't be nervous; I'm rooting for you from the bottom of my heart. The sky is the limit, but I'd be happy if you just get 1 or 2 more points than on the first test. I don't want to add any extra pressure, but at this point, if you don't get a high score, there's not much I can do for you. The scoring system is the same. Give yourself 0 points for each "a," 1 point for each "b," and 3 points for each "c" answer. Remember to answer the questions thinking with a Latino mind.

1. You have to buy a shirt for a job interview. You go to your favorite department store and you find out that they have only three colors left: lightning yellow, radioactive green, and flamingo pink. What would you do?
    a. Go to a different store.
    b. Tell the manager you *need* a royal purple shirt, and he has to find one for you.

c. Ask if they can quickly tailor these three shirts into one amazing garment.

2. What's the best phrase you'd use to describe Latino cuisine?
   a. "I don't know if you can call tortillas and chilies *cuisine.*"
   b. "Think of it as nature's broom."
   c. "So nice, it burns you twice!"

3. Your twenty-five-year-old son comes home in a brand-new sports car, wearing an expensive suit and a gold watch. What's the first thing you say?
   a. "You got a new job!"
   b. "Try not to max out all your credit cards."
   c. Nothing. You grab your baseball bat and threaten him until he promises to quit his gang.

4. What is *ropa vieja?*
   a. Is this a Spanish-language course? Don't know, don't care.
   b. Fancifully called "old rags," it's a traditional Latino dish of stewed beef.
   c. The only thing in your closet.

5. You come home one night. As soon as you open the door, you find your whole family has gathered to confront you about your gambling problem. How do you react?
   a. "I can't believe I'm putting all of you through this . . . I'm [sob] so sorry!"

b. "I figured there was a one-in-ten chance it would come to this."

c. "I bet a hundred dollars you can't make me quit—who's in?"

Results:

0 to 5 points: You think of yourself as practical, realistic, logical, and efficient, and worst of all, you think these are virtues. If you have travel plans to visit Latin America, get your money back—you'll never survive your trip.

6 to 12 points: You are doing well, but it's not enough. The contractors fixing your roof still hate you. It's time to go full throttle into the Latino world.

13 to 15 points: I think you are very close to being ready for your mustache and sombrero. Remember, though, your still-Anglo neighbors might become envious or even hostile when they see your new lifestyle.

PART 3

LANGUAGE AND MEDIA

CHAPTER 33

Talk to Me and I Will Tell You If You Are Latino

I've heard it said that if you speak three languages, you are trilingual, if you speak two, you are bilingual, and if you speak one, you are American. Nevertheless, if you want to understand Latinos, one of the most valuable and essential tools you need is a mastery of our vocabulary. I don't mean the Spanish language itself, but rather the colloquialisms and idioms in which we really have our conversations. Before we get to these phrases, there are some myths and truths to weigh.

Myth #1: Latinos talk really loud.
It is true. When I call my Anglo friends, they often ask me: "What's with all the screaming? Are you mad at me?" and I'm just saying *hello*. Why is that? A linguistics professor explained the Latinos' higher volume as the result of a greater presence of open vowels within the Spanish language—primarily *a* and *o*. The idea is that Spanish speakers would have to open our mouths wider than, for example, English speakers, and this makes Latinos yell. I can personally deny that theory based on the experi-

ence of Rodrigo Flores, a friend of mine who fractured his jaw playing basketball. His treatment consisted of four months of immobilization, and throughout the healing, he could only open his mouth enough to suck liquefied fruit through a straw, but Rodrigo kept yelling. This could be one of the main reasons why Latinos can't keep a secret: we don't know how to whisper, even with our jaws wired shut.

Myth #2: Latinos talk all at the same time.
A Latino always believes what he's saying is the most important part of the conversation, so he can't wait for someone else to finish a sentence. He also understands that everyone else feels the same way. We overlap each other, but the curious thing is that even when five Latinos are talking at once, every one of them understands what the other four are saying.

Truth #1: Latinos don't use the whole alphabet.
After years of sacrifice and making do with too little, Latinos have learned to get by without all the letters in the alphabet. Nowadays, the letter *s* at the end of a word doesn't exist for us. Latinos don't pronounce it, and in most cases it's not even written. The letter *s* is very important in proper Spanish. No wonder Anglos struggle to understand Latinos. Even if you learned Spanish, you couldn't hold a conversation with us. I've seen a lot of Anglo tourists in and around Miami Beach, baffled, trying to understand why a Latino valet just handed them their car keys and said *mucha gracia*, which literally means "very funny," instead of *muchas gracias*, meaning "thank you very much."

Truth #2: Every Latin American country speaks its own version of Spanish.

Beyond different accents, you have different *words*. It's not my intention to dig deeply into the differences between the Spanish spoken by Mexicans, Cubans, Puerto Ricans, and so on, but there are a few important things for you to know, a few weird idiomatic details that could easily drive you crazy if you are not prepared for them.

Mexicans have a particular word they use to end most of their sentences: *guey*, which means "dude." The thing is, they use the word *guey* almost in every situation. And to top it all off, it's pronounced "way." So you can see the silly situations this could lead to.

"Which way goes to the hotel?"

"Which *guey*? You can all go to the hotel."

"We don't know the way."

"You don't have to know any *guey*, you can just go there."

"No way!"

"Yes *guey*!"

Latinos from Cuba, on the other hand, use *chico* or *chica*—young boy or young girl—with every phrase that comes out of their mouths. Where an Anglo might say, "Come on, man," the Cuban says, *"Oye, chico."* And they use it for everything: *"Tu sabes, chico"*; *"Mira, chico"*; *"Déjame, chico"* ("You know, chico"; "Look, chico"; "Let me go, chico"). Therefore, if you converse with a Cuban, you shouldn't feel silly when he calls you "Chico"— even if you're seventy-five.

Finally, Puerto Rican Latinos change the letter *r* to *l* when pronouncing certain words, which totally drives you up the wall. *"Me voy a bañar"* ("I'm going to take a shower") is said *"Me voy a bañal." "Las cosas van a cambiar"* ("Things are going to change") is *"Las cosas van a cambial." "Esto es una mierda"* ("This is shit") is pronounced *"Esto es una miellda."*

To make things even more complicated, due to the cultural mixing over the last decade, you might encounter a Latino who has adopted idioms from different countries. If a Latino valet shouts something like: *"Guey! Vas a parkeal, chico?"* there's no doubt what that means: keep driving!

Dropping some letters from the alphabet, switching out others, and introducing silly forms of address are just minor abnormalities to be found in any living language. When you add to Spanish the powerful forces of immigration and assimilation, a fresh linguistic hell breaks loose:

- "Aplástale a las *brecas!*" (Hit the *brakes!*)
- "Qué pasa, *broder?*" (What's up, *brother?* If he's Puerto Rican, he'd pronounce it *"brodel."*)
- "Se acabaron los *confleys.*" (We're running out of *Corn Flakes.*)
- "No *cuitees* que vas ganando." (Don't you *quit* now that you're winning.)
- "Le diste una *chaineada* a tu carro." (You *shined* your car.)
- "*Chécate* esto!" (*Check* this out!)
- "Yo te *chuteo.*" (I *shoot* you.)
- "Quiero *dropearme* de la escuela." (I want to *drop out* of school.)
- "Esa película me *friqueó.*" (That movie *freaked* me out.)
- "Tengo que pagar mi *íncontas.*" (I must pay my *income tax.*)
- "Se me olvido *sainear* el cheque." (I forgot to *sign* the check.)
- "Puedes *yompearme* el carro?" (Would you *jump-start* my car?)

- "Voy a tirar todo al *yonque.*" (I'm going to throw it all to the *junkyard.*)

Dear English language: Be afraid, be very afraid. The Latinos are coming. Don't worry, we won't kill you, but your face might get rearranged, *guey.*

CHAPTER 34

ANGLO ENTERTAINMENT INDUSTRY
TARGETING LATINOS

Truth: Latinos are an important demographic within U.S. society.

I've spent just ten years of my professional life in this market, but I've seen how things have started to change. I normally go to a lot of auditions; that's how most of us actors get our jobs—unless we are big names. I have so many scripts piled up in my living room that I feel in part responsible for the deforestation of the Amazon. One thing I've noticed in the past couple of years is that many producers are willing to change the character they are auditioning for—they will consider making him Latino, if it makes sense to do so, in an attempt to attract a wider demographic.

I played a small role in *Basic* with John Travolta and Samuel L. Jackson. When I auditioned, my character was Anglo, but they changed it for me—and renamed him "Castro." I guess nobody would have bought the character if I played him as "Patrick." Besides that, the original casting for the role I play in the USA Network drama series *In Plain Sight* was developed for an African-American baseball player, whose name, as you might have guessed, was not "Raphael Ramirez."

Myth: Immigrants are taking American jobs.
For the last twenty years, Anglos have liked to believe that was a fact. Well, it's not. China and India are *taking* American jobs, we are just *doing* American jobs . . . in America. When the Japanese auto industry took the market by storm with their affordable, fuel-efficient cars, nobody tried to deport Japanese immigrants. Everybody seems to have adapted over time. Well . . . massive bailouts notwithstanding. And if you are an Anglo actor reading this, you can always audition for the smuggler, drug dealer, and gangster roles if you want. But my point doesn't stop there. I will take it much further: immigrants have given Anglos in the entertainment business hundreds of jobs. How can this be? Many of the hit TV shows that you've embraced and loved throughout the last years are nothing but ideas stolen from Latinos. You see, there was a time when ingenious Latino writers were eagerly looking for jobs in Hollywood, and they'd do anything to get a meeting with a TV network executive. If you want a TV network to buy your concept for a show, you must do a "pitch," which is basically explaining your idea and how they are going to nail big ratings with it. In my experience, when you are trying to sell your vision, they're always thinking the same thing: "How could we do this show *without* the guy pitching it?" What did the network executives do? They bought the ideas, only to use the titles. Without further ado, here are the TV titles that wound up being hits, with their original pitches:

- *House*
  Working out of his home, a cranky *curandero* makes illogical diagnoses and prescribes seemingly insane treatments, which always work.
- *American Idol*
  An illegal immigrant marries an attractive Anglo woman, becomes a U.S. citizen, and attains heroic status back in his hometown of Metlatonoc, Mexico.
- *30 Rock*
  A mariachi group decides to switch styles and they end up becoming rock 'n' roll legends.
- *Desperate Housewives*
  Four Latinas search every dance club in town looking for their good-for-nothing husbands.
- *24*
  A real-time docudrama about a Puerto Rican couple and their twenty-two kids.
- *Dancing with the Stars*
  A Colombian drug "mule" accidentally punctures one of the baggies she was trying to swallow. As a half pound of cocaine courses through her, she exits her body and floats into the sky, where she does the Macarena with Ritchie Valens, Frida Kahlo, and Tito Puente.
- *The West Wing*
  Two Cuban brothers fight over who gets the last piece of chicken.
- *The Office*
  An undocumented worker conspires to break into an INS office to steal the answers to the U.S. citizenship test, only to find out later that they are posted online.

- *Friends*
  A group of coyotes (professional smugglers) from El Paso help some Mexicans to cross the U.S. border.
- *The Amazing Race*
  A continuation of *Friends*, things heat up once a Border Patrol officer starts pursuing their van.
- *Deal or No Deal*
  A continuation of *The Amazing Race*, the coyotes attempt to negotiate a bribe with a Border Patrol officer.

CHAPTER 35

Soap Operas in Spanish —*La Novela*

Cristián de la Fuente

I was the lead guy in the first series produced in Spanish by Jennifer Lopez. Finally, I was treated like a star. So here's my trailer. No, not the big one. Mine was the small pickup on the back.

In the twenty-first century, the media has become a fundamental part of everyday life for everyone all around the globe—except for the Amish. Between cable TV, newspapers, and magazines, you would have to be a space alien to be unaware of the news. E-mail and text messaging have eclipsed communication by regular telephone and mail. Cable TV companies offer hundreds of channels, in every language, live from everywhere—and I'm talking about the basic package here; I can only dream about what the premium deals get you.

Anglos—including those living in a cabin in Lickskillet Holler, Kentucky, who haven't seen a Latino even once in their lives—have access to the Latino world thanks to the Spanish-language soap operas on cable. Three decades ago, we couldn't have dreamed that a Latino, an Anglo, an Eskimo, and Big Foot would all be watching *Yo Sé Que La Niñera Es La Hija De Tu Abuelo Millonario* (*I Know the Nanny Is Your Rich Grandpa's Daughter*) at the same time. It's said that a little knowledge can be a dangerous thing, so let's make sure we ask the right questions about *novelas*—for example, "How accurately do they reflect the real Latino experience?"

Myth #1: *Novelas* represent Latino life accurately.
This is false. Latinos love to engage in the drama, but we know it's just entertainment. Sadly, not everybody is aware of that. I have some Anglo friends who are taking Spanish lessons, and they watch *novelas* in order to practice pronunciation. They have asked me: "Why do Latinas cry all day long? I feel sorry for you, your marriage must be unbearable." Anglos also tend to believe that every Latino is Mexican, because the Spanish-language networks cater to their largest demographic. That's like watching Lifetime and thinking all Americans are middle-aged white women with alcoholic husbands.

Myth #2: *Novelas* are more melodramatic and ridiculous than American soap operas.

This is true. I've watched Anglo soap operas, and they are so boring. A whole episode and nobody accidentally shot the wrong person, only to find out he was her son? Nobody got pregnant by someone in an elaborate disguise? Why would you watch this? Latinos need to see somebody else suffering more than themselves. When we watch American soap operas, we feel like the characters could be comforted by watching our real lives.

Myth #3: A *novela* actor overexaggerates.

There's no such thing as a *"novela* actor." There is such a thing as an actor who can't get parts in movies, sitcoms, dramas, plays, or musicals. When the casting director of a musical asks if you can "tone it down," it's probably time to go back to *novelas.*

Myth #4: Anglos wouldn't understand a *novela* even if they understand Spanish.

That's true, but it can be fixed. Once everybody in your house is sleeping, fix yourself a big bag of extra-butter microwave popcorn and get a comfy seat in front of your television. There are several Hispanic networks, but using the on-screen guide, you happen to find Univision first. You don't understand a word, but you get the story. There's a murder, a betrayal, a horrendous accident, and a surprise pregnancy; a wealthy granny loses her memory while her good-looking eldest son goes blind; the respectable head of the household is having an affair with the insanely busty cook, who turns out to be none other than the daughter he lost twenty years ago. This is not a synopsis of the season, it's the first five minutes of one episode.

You switch the channel to Telemundo. Their *novela* is basically the same, with the addition of a gypsy caravan.

Despite the awkwardly fake situations, the bizarre, over-wrought performances, and the inexplicably loud fights, something magical happens. You can't help but keep watching it. Five minutes later, a tear runs down your cheek when you see María decide to have her baby, despite being single, unemployed, quadriplegic, and a werewolf. The miracle has begun for you.

Thirty minutes later, you have finished the popcorn, a six-pack of beer, and two boxes of Kleenex. Nobody knows what their secret is, but *novelas* are the king of TV among Hispanic viewers in the United States. Even though everybody knows María will marry the heartthrob millionaire's son in the last episode, no matter how hard his snobby girlfriend tries to stop them, we couldn't bear to miss a single episode.

Final advice: Once you have finished your thorough analysis of *novelas*, you should use parental controls to disable the Hispanic TV networks on your cable box. You must continue on your path of study, and not remain in one place, no matter how much you enjoy it—just as you do not make kindergarten crafts with glitter and glue in high school. What was that? Okay, you're right. I got you into this, so it seems to be my fault somehow. Go ahead, you can keep watching *El Amor de María* until the end.

CHAPTER 36

BREAKING INTO HOLLYWOOD
THROUGH THE FRONT DOOR

Why have Latinos finally been able to break through in Hollywood? In order to answer that question, we have to go back to
the beginning. When Anthony Quinn, born in Mexico in 1915,
was starring in *Lawrence of Arabia* in 1962, it was extremely
unusual to see a Latino actor playing a non-Latino character. I
mean, it was very unusual to see a Latino in a starring role.
I mean, it was unusual to see a Latino working in the industry
outside of catering. On television, you had watched Cuban-born
Desi Arnaz since 1951, but he was married in real life to the
show's creator and star. Not until 1978 did we see Ricardo Mon-
talban, also born in Mexico, play the main character on the TV
hit *Fantasy Island.* Later, the Cuban-born Maria Conchita Alonso
would costar in *The Running Man* with Arnold Schwarzenegger,
fellow Cuban Andy García would appear in *The Untouchables,*
and Puerto Rican Raúl Juliá would shine in *Kiss of the Spider
Woman.*

The truth about Latino roles. Besides these few exceptions, most Latinos roles have been bit parts that fit four basic characteristics:

1. They are involved in some kind of illegal activity, like weapons sales or drug trafficking.

2. They live in bad neighborhoods—even though weapons sales and drug trafficking are very lucrative.

3. They look filthy, raunchy, and thuggish.

4. When two Latino characters are by themselves in a room, they converse using English. Later, when they interact with non-Latino characters, they will slip in a few words of Spanish.
   If an Anglo in the audience didn't have any Latinos living nearby—and twenty-five years ago, it was still possible—all he would have is the message sent by the media: "Beware of these people." Thank God today the media has evolved, along with society, of course. Latino characters are not just gang members anymore. Now they are businessmen and millionaires—for example, large-scale smugglers, international diamond thieves, and world-class con artists.
   One way or the other, we made it. Today we not only see Latino actors starring in movies and TV series, but we also get nominated to big Anglo awards like the Oscars and the Emmys. Hollywood has definitely opened the doors to Latino actors. Why did that happen? Did Anglos finally recognize our talent and dedication? Don't

be insane; the truth is that Latino actors help rake in a lot of money at the box office these days. Here's how the Hollywood decision-making process works:

Step #1: A foreign actor is famous overseas, and his mere presence is guaranteed to make a box-office hit in his home country. Despite the thousands of talented Latino actors struggling to make it in Hollywood, this actor's name comes up in a meeting—due entirely to the fact that the studio head happened to read a one-paragraph article about him in *Variety* five minutes ago in the bathroom.

Step #2: The marketing department calculates that there are three potential audiences: immigrants from his country who know his name well; Latinos in general, who are just happy to see a Latino in a movie; and Anglo women who have read about how handsome he is in *Entertainment Weekly*.

Step #3: It comes to light that this actor doesn't speak a word of English. No one wants to shoot down the studio head's big idea, so plans are quickly made to bring him over and teach him English, and if he can't learn, to rewrite his part as a mime.

On the other end of the spectrum, there are many Latino actors who can play an Anglo character flawlessly. You may recognize them by their Spanish names—if you are patient enough to reach the end of the scrolling credits—but you would otherwise have no idea. The truth is that—in most cases—the role's title is something like "man on the street #1" or "girl passing by" or "policeman #22," but keep in mind that doesn't say "*Latino* policeman #22," so that's an Anglo character, at least in my book.

Honestly, I don't know why it took Latino actors so long to start getting Anglo roles. Surprisingly, there was no hesitation

XLV FESTIVAL INTERNACIONAL DE LA CANCIÓN
VIÑA DEL MAR - CHILE 2004

Cristián de la Fuente

The first time I danced on TV was not on *Dancing with the Stars* but in a famous Latino music festival called *Festival de Viña del Mar* in Chile. Here with me is Juan Gabriel, teaching me his famous dance, *Noa Noa*. If you don't know who he is, you're definitely an Anglo. Google him.

the other way around. Al Pacino is a great actor; I love his work. He played a Cuban in *Scarface* and a Puerto Rican in *Carlito's Way*, and in both cases his acting was outstanding, but his accents sucked. I think no Latino actor has ever spoken about this issue openly before, probably because Mr. Pacino can destroy a career with one phone call. But if we are going to coexist in this country, it's time to start being honest with each other.

NOTE: If, by chance, you happen to be a friend of Al Pacino, I hope this comment doesn't ruin my chances of working with him, and I'm not talking about mowing his lawn. Unless he wants me to, of course, let's not kid ourselves.

CHAPTER 37

THE REAL MEANINGS BEHIND LATINO SONGS

Maybe the easiest way to get to know a culture is through its music. Our musical history shares our experiences and messages across generations and cultural boundaries. The first question is: What do Latinos listen to?

Myth #1: Latinos listen to ranchera, Tejano, regional, and other kinds of Mexican music.
False. Only Mexicans listen to Mexican music exclusively—and not all of them, either. Latinos love all kinds of music, so long as the rhythm is a call to action. I might mean dancing, I might mean more, who knows? Which brings us to the next myth.

Myth #2: All Latino songs have sexual lyrics.
Mostly true. Latino lyrics are to music what *novelas* are to television. It's always drama, emotion, and getting women to let their guard down—then boom! I got you, babe. In all honesty, maybe

all music has been created for that purpose. The renowned singer and songwriter Joan Manuel Serrat, born in Spain, once said, "In life, everything men do is to get women." Even if the seduction is not overt, it might be covered by the next myth.

Myth #3: Latino songs have subliminal messages, hidden between the lyrics.

This is true. If we take a close look at the songs and we know how to interpret their meanings, we'll have a priceless tool for understanding Latinos. And that's what I'm about to do. I've intentionally chosen some romantic songs where, apparently, the lyrics speak of lost loves. Within each of them, the hidden message takes a completely distinct path. The listeners love the song we hear, but unconsciously our brains get the other message, filling in the blanks on their own.

You won't find a songwriter at a press conference explaining what he wanted to say when he wrote, "The flower of your aura embedded my soul fueled with desire." First, artists don't like to give explanations for their work. Second, he doesn't have the remotest guess what the hell he was trying to say when he wrote that song. It may have been the only rhyme he could think of at the time. The following are fragments of songs recorded by successful Latino singers, followed by their literal English translations, and finally the subliminal message I believe made each song such a hit.

"Tu Amor o tu desprecio" ("Your Love or Your Hate")
Artist: Marco Antonio Solís, from Mexico

Tal vez es un error hoy de mi parte el aferrarme a esto tan bonito

(It might be my mistake to hold on to this beauty thing)

Pero no soy capaz ni de enfrentarte y decirte que yo no te necesito . . .
(But I'm not even capable of facing you to tell you that I no longer need you)

Apparently, the song is talking about an ending love, but it could easily be the story of an illegal immigrant who got married to an American citizen to get his green card. The phrase "to tell you that I no longer need you" is at the very least suspicious. Of course, he has obtained legal status! That was all he wanted from her.

"A Medio Vivir" ("Half Living")
Artist: Ricky Martin, from Puerto Rico

Ese primer día que nos vimos desnudos, y siempre pensé la vida debe de continuar
(That first day we saw each other naked, and I always thought life must go on)

Pero sin tí todo se quedó por la mitad
(But without you everything stood incomplete)

Can you see the subliminal message here? I wonder how many love stories have risen between doctors and applicants for citizenship. In case you didn't know, in order to get legal residency in the United States (the step before citizenship), the applicant must go through a mandatory medical examination. That kind of intimacy can leave emotional scars, and this man doesn't care about his green card if he's not able to keep seeing the health care professional who inspected his private parts.

"Ciega, Sordomuda" ("Blind, Deaf and Mute")
Artist: Shakira, from Colombia

Bruta, ciega, sordomuda; torpe, traste y testaruda
(Dumb, blind, deaf and mute; clumsy, junk and pigheaded)

Es todo lo que he sido, por tí me he convertido
(That's all I've been, because of you I've become one)

Shakira has made the crossover, and she's been singing in English for years now. This song was composed when she still didn't sing in English. It seems like an innocent song about a girl who becomes blind because of love, but the subliminal message speaks to all those Latinos who are trying to learn English. When struggling with a new language, we all feel "Dumb, blind, deaf and mute, clumsy, junk and pigheaded." She must have written it when she started to learn English herself.

"Usted Abusó" ("You Took Advantage of Me")
Artist: Celia Cruz, from Cuba

Usted abusó, sacó provecho de mí, abusó
(You took advantage of me, you harassed me, you took advantage of me)

Sacó partido de mí, abusó, de mi cariño usted abusó
(You took advantage of me, you harassed me, from my fondness you abused)

The main character of this story feels abused because she trusted another human being, presumably with her love. Yet any girl who listens to this song will recall that single date in which a Latino took her to a cheap restaurant, split the bill, and instead of trying to kiss her, he asked her for a loan. It wasn't her heart he plundered, it was her forty dollars.

"La Bilirrubina" ("The Bilirubin")
Artist: Juan Luis Guerra, from the Dominican Republic

Y me inyectaron suero de colores y me sacaron la radiografía
(And they injected me with colored serum and they took a radiography of my body)

Y me diagnosticaron mal de amores al ver mi corazón como latía
(And they diagnosed "Love illness" seeing the way my heart was beating)

I saved the best for last, a simple song about a man who's lovesick. Any Latino who has been in an emergency room without heath insurance knows these lyrics have a completely different meaning, which creates an instant bond with the listener. We all know how the medical system mistreats these people. Pay attention to the lyrics. This man went to the hospital, they injected him with a "colored serum"—probably one past its expiration date—and they took a radiography. That was the best treatment they were willing to give to somebody without insurance.

They couldn't make an accurate diagnosis with these limited tools, so they told him he was *in love*, when in reality he was having tachycardia caused by a hypertrophic cardiomyopathy. Sadly, the triple bypass he needed wasn't covered by the public health system. It was better for him to die at home, thinking he was in love. Definitely an impassioned protest song against the medical establishment, hidden behind a catchy rhythm. This song was a tremendous success that skyrocketed Juan Luis Guerra's musical career, but if the government had noticed his subversive message, the story might have turned out a very different way.

Since the beginning of this century, U.S. government agencies have been double-checking the lyrics, titles, and even the names of the musical groups intending to break into the Latino music market in the United States. The agencies' goal is to detect any subliminal messages and prevent them from reaching the Latino population. The first group banned was the Chilean band Los Ilegales (The Illegals), whose plans for touring the States went down the drain when their visas were denied for life, as a precaution.

CHAPTER 38

Latino Versions of Hollywood Blockbusters

Truth #1: Movies are not what they used to be.

Over the last couple of years, a record percentage of the big Hollywood openings have been nothing but remakes of old movies. With so much money at stake—we're talking about a budget of $100 million-plus per flick—nobody wants to take a risk. The remake gives the studio a sort of "free test" in the marketplace, because they know how well the original version worked. Producers are well aware that a remake guarantees a certain minimum number of people at the box office—unless it's *Waterworld* or *Gigli*—in which case it's a maximum number.

Truth #2: Latinos go to the movies.

Latinos are not afraid to spend on entertainment, sometimes at extravagant levels. The revenue from Latino moviegoers increases year after year, a trend that has caught the attention of the film industry.

The conclusion: Following the advice of "marketing experts," the movie studios decided to remake a series of classic movies, specially tailored to appeal to Latino audiences. They assembled a creative team of professional writers from several Latin American backgrounds to choose, adapt, and rewrite blockbuster scripts to be produced and released into the market as soon as possible. Unfortunately, this team was disbanded a couple of months later, because they spent all of their brainstorming time drinking beer, holding burping contests, and making advances toward female personnel. Fortunately for history, the few synopses they did create were found stuck to the bottom of a pizza box as their offices were being cleared out.

Original title & release year: *Mission: Impossible* (1996)
New synopsis: Two newly arrived immigrants decide to enroll in a public school to learn English. It turns out to be really difficult. They have a studying montage, but even that doesn't work. Meanwhile, they both marry rich widows, get citizenship, and multiply their huge fortunes, but they still can't conjugate the past perfect continuous tense. **New genre:** Romantic Comedy.

Original title & release year: *Kramer vs. Kramer* (1979)
New working title: *Gonzalez vs. Gonzalez vs. Gonzalez*
New synopsis: A Latino married couple decides to call it off and get a divorce. They agree on everything but one detail: their son, seven-year-old Jose. Neither wants to keep the boy, because they both have children from previous marriages—she has six, and he has eleven. While each sues the other for enforced custody, Jose sues them both for emancipation and back child support. **Genre:** Courtroom Drama.

Original title & release year: *Titanic* (1997)

New synopsis: May be one of the studio's most ambitious productions: a world-class giant raft, popularly believed to be unsinkable, leaves the island of Cuba on its maiden voyage, carrying hundreds of men, women, and children in a hopeful journey to a better future in the United States. Bad weather threatens the vessel while "Onei" and "Regla," the sweet starring couple, hunt for a private place to consummate their passion—which is impossible aboard a flat raft with no doors, walls, or roof whatsoever. Thirty-five miles off the U.S. coast, the raft strikes an abandoned Soviet naval mine. The crew valiantly tries to avoid the collision, but it's too late, and the raft gets blown to pieces. Some of the passengers manage to grab big chunks of wood to keep themselves afloat, but Onei and Regla decide to make love under the water, which is the first privacy they've had. In a big finale, a coast guard patrol rescues the survivors and takes them to the mainland. Onei is not so lucky, because he's run over by a Jet Ski and dies without having the chance to reach the U.S. coast. The beautiful Regla makes it to Miami, but she'll never Jet Ski again.

Genre: Historical Drama.

Original title & release year: *The Lord of the Rings: The Return of the King* (2003)

New synopsis: A Puerto Rican jewelry smuggler was betrayed in New York and sentenced to spend a long time behind bars. Today, "Daddy King" is a free man again, and he has returned for his payback. Those who betrayed him know there's no place to hide—since the day of his release, the New York streets have been the scene of bloody fights, dead bodies in alleys, pile-up car crashes, kidnappings, arsons, and overwhelmed law enforcement officers unable to put an end to the chaos. To tell the truth, it's been just like any other day in New York.

New genre: Gangster.

Original title & release year: *E. T.* (1982)

New synopsis: It's the 1940s in the United States when Ernesto Torres crosses the border. A seven-year-old girl discovers Ernesto in her backyard, gets scared, and screams as if she'd seen an alien. Ernesto tries to calm her in Spanish, but for the little girl he speaks a language from outer space. When she calms down, they share some Chiclets and she hides him in her house. Finally, the whole family adopts Ernesto, but the rumors have spread around town. The authorities want to know what kind of strange creature they are harboring. E.T. decides he had better go back to his world, so a group of children help Ernesto make it back to the border. In a tearful farewell scene, he pronounces the famous phrase: *"Ernesto Torres llamar a casa"* (E.T. phone home).

CHAPTER 39

Differences Between Anglos and Latinos, Part 3

You have read a lot of truths and myths about language and media, but how much have you absorbed? Here are some situations in which our theories can be seen in practice:

- *Situation A.* You are on your way to a friend's house in a historic part of the city. The neighborhood is full of tourists taking pictures and admiring the sights. At some point, one man stops you and asks something in a foreign language. How do you respond?
  - **Anglo guide:** Says, "I'm sorry, I don't understand."
  - **Latino guide:** Says, "What are you speaking, Puerto Rican?"
  - **Anglo guide:** Says, "Let's find a tourist information booth."
  - **Latino guide:** Says, "Let's find a peep show booth!"
  - **Anglo guide:** Calls his wife to say he'll be late because he has to help somebody find his destination.

- **Latino guide:** Points west, because he is remembering something hilarious that happened in that direction.
- *Situation B.* You have been following a soap opera throughout the season. You are five minutes away from the end of the last episode and, obviously, you are in tears. Your husband opens the door and he tells you he has another woman in his life and he wants a divorce. What do you do?
  - **Anglo soap opera lover:** Says, "How can you do this to me?"
  - **Latina soap opera lover:** Says, "How can you do this to *my finale!*"
  - **Anglo soap opera lover:** Starts throwing everything within reach at his head.
  - **Latina soap opera lover:** Starts throwing everything within reach at his head . . . during the commercials.
  - **Anglo soap opera lover:** Doesn't say a word, starts packing her stuff, and swears he will never see her again.
  - **Latina soap opera lover:** Doesn't say a word, as she *really* needs to pay attention to the TV right now.
- *Situation C.* Your best friend died in a car accident. He was young and full of life. At the funeral service, somebody starts playing a joyful song. How do you react?
  - **Anglo mourner:** Finds where the music is coming from and turns it off.
  - **Latina mourner:** Starts dancing sexy—and turns everyone on.
  - **Anglo mourner:** Gives that person a killer look.
  - **Latina mourner:** Gives that person a killer show.
  - **Anglo mourner:** Yells, "Please respect the deceased!"

- **Latina mourner:** Yells, "The widow is a great dancer, too!"
- *Situation D.* A car is rushing through the streets of a quiet neighborhood. Inside the vehicle are four male subjects, who ride with their bodies hanging halfway out of the windows, and all of them carry heavy machine guns. There's a stop sign at the end of the block. They open fire on it until the sign is destroyed, as they laugh hysterically.
  - **Anglo viewer:** Says, "This movie is great! I've never seen that kind of action!"
  - **Latino viewer:** Says, "This neighborhood is terrible! That should not happen outside of a movie."
  - **Anglo viewer:** Says, "I guess we'll see a police car chasing them any minute."
  - **Latino viewer:** Says, "I guess we'll never see a police car. They are afraid to come here."
  - **Anglo viewer:** Thinks, "I would've liked my uncle to see this film. He loves action movies!"
  - **Latino viewer:** Thinks, "I hope no one saw my uncle in the passenger seat."
- *Situation E. Language—Autobiography.* Let's say your life is pretty interesting. You decide to write a book recounting all of your experiences. What would be the ideal title?
  - **Anglo writer:** *My Life*
  - **Latino writer:** *You Call This a Life?*
  - **Anglo writer:** *Always Looking Up*
  - **Latino writer:** *Always Looking Out*
  - **Anglo writer:** *Resilience*
  - **Latino writer:** *Residence*

CHAPTER 40

THE *NOVELA* ON-SCREEN KISS

As an actor who has starred in a handful of *novelas*, I'm usually asked about the kissing. How does that feel? Is it real or not? And so on. I decided to compile in this book a selection of the best questions I heard regarding this issue and answer them here.

- Are the kisses real or are they computer-generated?
  Do you think Latino production companies are like Dreamworks? We can't afford craft services, much less computer-generated images. And why would we do it anyway? It's just a kiss, not a space mission to the sun.
- Do you feel something when you kiss the actress?
  I can tell you, it's not the same that I feel when I kiss my beloved wife. Hi, honey, I love you so much! At the same time, you are still a man and a woman, made of flesh and sometimes bone, if you know what I mean.
- What happens when the woman you have to kiss has bad breath?

Cristián de la Fuente

This picture was taken during a live TV interview in Chile. They were asking me if it's true that I have a pink computer. News flies nowadays.

You kiss her anyway, because it is the scent of a paycheck. If you are friends with the actress, you can guess what she had for lunch.

- Is it true that kissing scenes usually require multiple takes?

  They require more takes if the actress is hot and the director is a pal.

- What do you do when you just had a fight with your Latina costar and you have to act a love scene with her?

  She does the same thing as with her husband—fakes it. At least with me it's a three-minute scene, not a lifetime with a lazy bum.

- How do you know if it's okay to use the tongue while you are kissing?

  I never really had to think about it—you'd be surprised how often Latina actresses take the initiative.

- Does the kissing sometimes lead to something more after the shoot is finished?

  It depends, of course, but this question answers itself if you read the tabloids. You ever notice how often Hollywood couples start dating right after they work together? They say opportunity makes the thief.

- Does your wife get jealous when you kiss another woman on-screen?

  My wife doesn't get jealous. She's a grown-up who understands that's the way I make a living, and that there's a difference between an on-screen kiss and a real kiss. But she'll kick me under the seat anyway, for reasons known only to her.

CHAPTER 41

So You're in Love with a Latino Heartthrob . . .

First of all, let's define heartthrob. The Merriam-Webster dictionary says: *Heartthrob: a usually renowned man (as an entertainer) noted for his sex appeal.* That's a good start, but I'd say there is much more to it. Not every good-looking Latino actor qualifies to be placed in this category. Let's establish the requirements in more detail:

1. He has to be good-looking.
    And not just to his mother. He has to have symmetrical features, the right angles, not too round, not too square—he should look like a *matador*.

2. He has to be well built.
    He has to go to the gym, train regularly, and have muscle. The prison yard doesn't count as a gym!

3. He has to be tough, yet sensitive.
    He needs to be the man you see and think, "Wow, I

hope to be next to him if an earthquake strikes." On the other hand, when his best friend dies in a motorcycle accident, he should stare at the sky, looking for answers, as a tear runs down his cheek.

4. He has to dress accordingly.
   He could be good-looking, but it is negated by sandals with socks. He has to wear clothes from a recognizable brand: cool, hip, and modern. You must pay special attention to his watch—if it's a fake, he's a fake. A heartthrob is not afraid of showing off his wealth, even if he's poor.

5. He has to smell like roses.
   Heartthrobs look like Vin Diesel, but they smell like Liberace. They could run the New York City Marathon in a tuxedo without sweating.

6. You can get him in bed, but he'll never spend the night.
   If regular men don't like to spoon after sex, heartthrobs don't even want you in the apartment. They *need* to be by themselves at night, as part of a process I call the "Cinderella condition": at midnight, the carriage turns into a pumpkin. How do you think they manage to look that good all day? They put creams and mud masks and cucumber jellies over their faces; they put leave-in conditioner in their hair, and wear a shower cap to contain it; they put lotion on their hands and wear dishwashing gloves to bed. The combined effect looks like something out of *Mars Attacks!*

Getting the heartthrob beauty treatment with my daughter.

For a Latino man to qualify as a heartthrob, he has to comply with all six points. Otherwise, he may be hot, he may even be the man of your dreams, but he's not a heartthrob.

Just for fun, let's say you've beaten the odds and actually found a Latino who meets all six heartthrob requirements. Naturally, you are deeply in love with him. You couldn't bear to blow this dream romance, so let's cover some dos and don'ts.

TOP FIVE THINGS YOU SHOULD *NEVER* DO WHEN YOU ARE WITH A HEARTTHROB:

5. Don't ask for an autograph. He's been tricked into signing marriage licenses before, and he's learned his lesson.

4. Don't say, "I would do anything for you," because he might ask you to bring him a pizza, clean his apartment, and leave.

3. Don't point your finger at him and shout to your friends, "Is he hot or what?" He will think you are propositioning him as a group, and he will be disappointed to learn otherwise.

2. Don't wait for him to notice your presence. You are not for him, and you know it. If you are Pamela Anderson, Beyoncé, or Penélope Cruz, please disregard this message.

1. If things go wrong, don't spend the rest of the night wondering what you could have done differently. By the time you start questioning yourself, he's already home shaving his chest.

HOW TO CONQUER A LATINO HEARTTHROB.

This is not an easy task. What can you do to catch such elusive prey? I can't give you a formula or an infallible set of pickup lines, but I can recommend some tactics that might help you.

1. As you walk by him, say to your friend, "He's hot, but not as hot as Javier Bardem." He'll become too depressed to shave his back or pluck his uni-brow, and in a few weeks he'll be easily attainable.

2. Find his best friend, who is usually ugly as hell, since heartthrobs don't like competition. You'll

have to sleep with the friend—I'm sorry, you can't skip that part—then tell them both that you are also developing feelings for the heartthrob, and you are mixed up. Now the heartthrob is in competition for you, even though he can't remember ever being attracted to you, and to lose to his ugly friend would be unthinkable and humiliating.

3. Tell him you love the carnival, especially the house of mirrors—would he like to go?

4. Get him in your car and crash it, badly. I know it's kind of extreme, but it worked with Tom Cruise in *Vanilla Sky*.

CHAPTER 42

So You're Trying to Have a Civilized Conversation with a Latino ...

Latinos love to chat, and not just water cooler conversations about football standings—we're very open and straightforward, even when it comes to intimate topics. We'll improvise a hilarious reenactment of our recent hemorrhoids surgery, even if it's our first day on the job. We don't really need an important subject to philosophize about. Any Latino could talk for forty-five minutes about the weather, and by the end of it you would know everything about our family, hometown, and job history. When you're in a doctor's waiting room, there's nothing better than to meet a Latino. Funnier than a book, more vivid than HDTV, and more informative than WebMD—at least about the medical histories of all of our relatives.

You'd rarely find that shy Latino, the one who smiles rather than bursting out laughing, who listens to you before continuing to talk nonsense, and who doesn't subject you to every detail of his genealogical tree and the circumstances under which he entered the United States. Latinos know how to be heard, whether or not anyone is listening.

When you first meet a Latino face-to-face, the biggest challenge is, how do you carry on a dialogue? The key to these conversations is to recognize some common elements within Latino speech. They will help you know when to change the subject, when to listen, when to interrupt, and above all, when to slip out through the emergency exit.

IF THERE'S SOMETHING HARD TO DO, THE LATINO HAS DONE IT ALREADY.

Whether it's unarmed bear hunting or street racing a Ferrari, the Latino has done it. Despite the fact that he crossed the border from Mexico on foot, he considers himself a "citizen of the world." If it's about flying to the moon, he's first on the waiting list.

IF YOU HAVE A GOOD STORY TO SHARE, HE HAS A BETTER ONE.

If you've planted a tree, he's saved half the Amazon. If a shark has attacked you, he came from Cuba inside a whale. If you just lost a close relative, his entire home country was murdered last week. A philosophy professor developed the theory that this behavior is a Latino defense mechanism. After so many years of being discriminated against, we use it to keep our egos up. I don't buy it, since the professor's last name was Gonzalez, he took two and a half hours to explain his theory, and he took credit for all the ideas in *Star Wars*. Here's some advice: Don't try to compete, just say, "Wow! I've never heard something like that in my whole life!" As a bonus, you'll probably be telling the truth.

BACK IN HIS COUNTRY, HE WAS POWERFUL AND WEALTHY.

Everybody says we were in a better position before, but then why did we leave? Let's be honest, if you were the owner of a successful company, with a house in the country, a big mansion on the beach, expensive cars, and a luxury life, what would draw you to America and a job delivering pizzas . . . free pizza? It doesn't matter how silly the claims are, because nobody can *prove* you didn't own something. If every Cuban exile living in Miami had the land he claims back in his country, Cuba would be the eighth continent.

Every time we tell the story we add details, giving more footage to our properties, more zeros to our bank accounts, and more women to our legion of conquests. If two years ago he sounded like he was a computer entrepreneur, today he is "the Bill Gates of South America." The truth? He probably sold calculators door to door.

OUR CHILDREN ARE THE BEST IN THE WORLD.

To begin with, we take at least twenty minutes to mention our descendants—keep in mind each one of them has three to seven names—and another good hour to detail their natural gifts and blessings. I have a daughter, and when she messes things up, I can't even tell my wife. It would end up being my fault anyway, because we have developed an ability to reverse our kids' flaws into virtues. If our son is in jail, he's "taking some time to think about his future." If our daughter takes money in exchange for intimacy, she has "a head for business." If our teenager spray-paints public statues, he's "a political artist." If our five-year-old takes down the pants of a boy at school, she'll "probably be a doctor."

THE LATINO IS UNABLE TO LISTEN.

If it's true that Latinos don't listen, how are you supposed to be able to engage in a conversation with us? The answer is: we're not deaf, but we have what I like to call selective hearing. If you say, for instance: "The weather is so nice that I'm planning a fishing trip with the family next week, to spend some quality time together. I'd like to forget about business for a while." First, the Latino will finish whatever he was saying, which will take about twenty minutes. Then he'll come back to the important words in your statement: fishing, family, and business.

Fishing: He'll tell you about that time he caught the biggest fish in the Atlantic.

Family: He'll tell you about his son's passion for gold jewelry.

Business: He'll ask you to lend him some money for a business that can't go wrong.

Don't feel let down by his response, it could be worse. Imagine a conversation between two Latinos—it's not a dialogue, it's two monologues dueling like banjos. Finally, let me say that the key to communication is patience—*your* patience, of course, not his. Let him do most of the talking and try to agree, nodding once in a while . . . and don't worry about seeming insincere, he's not really paying much attention anyway. Thank god we have e-mail nowadays, the end of face-to-face conversation as we knew it. Although a Latino will also say he invented that, too— back in his country, twenty years ago.

CHAPTER 43

So You're an Anglo Actor Competing
Against a Latino for a Role . . .

I know this topic is too narrow for the audience of this book, but please humor me on this one, as it's an important issue to me personally. As I've stated several times before, it's hard for a Latino actor to get a job in this country. However, tables are turning and soon history will be rewritten . . . in Spanish. There will be a time, sooner rather than later, when Anglo actors will struggle to get a gig, because of us.

Before we begin, I have to apologize to my fellow Latino actors, because I'm about to reveal some key details and characteristics of our talents and skills. You must forgive me. If I sell enough books, I could stop going to auditions, at least for a while. That'd be less competition for you.

As a struggling Anglo actor, the first thing you have to do as you enter the audition waiting room is scan the competition. For instance: "I'm taller than this one, cuter than the other one, and I don't look as nervous as that guy biting his nails by the window." We all do that. Next, you have to identify the enemy—

the Latino actor. Don't worry, it's an easy task. He's the only one rehearsing his lines at the top of his lungs with a strange accent. Your first impression would be: "He is not going to make it." But be aware that the director may be on the lookout for some edgy character. That's why he's here. That's why you should become edgier than him, and you only have a couple of minutes to do it.

Option #1: Copy him. Repeat after him, trying to use the same accent. The script might say "jealousy," but you should say "yealousy."

Option #2: Say to him, "Didn't we meet the other night at Tom Cruise's party?" The Latino actor will say yes, even though he works as a stripper every night. Next, whisper, "That guy knows your sister . . ." Every Latino has a sister. ". . . And he told me she's hot in bed." Between the fight and the police arriving at the studio, you've eliminated almost all the competition. That role is yours.

Option #3: Tell him that the casting director was robbed last week by a Latino gang. Now when she sees a Latino, she calls the police immediately, but unless you have warrants—like for unpaid parking tickets or back child support—there's nothing to worry about.

Option #4: Prepare your best role. This is a risky one, but the payoff is great. You have to pose as the casting director and spread false information throughout the room. You will identify yourself and then go to the other actors one by one—since alerting the real casting director to what you are doing can't be good—saying to every one of them that you like him better than the others, and giving them a different callback time for the next day. Give the Latino actor a date for a week later, so he can prepare his second audition. Latinos are accustomed to callbacks that end up being suspended. It's the way they keep us waiting in line forever.

CHAPTER 44

TEST #3—HEY, MACARENA!

We are about to finish the part of the book about language and media. I hope by now you have realized how important it is to learn how to communicate appropriately with and within the Latino world. Because of that, I must test your Latino-ness for the third time.

1. You get home early and you find your house-keeper tied to a chair in the middle of the living room. What would you do?
   a. I would untie her and call the police. We must've been robbed.
   b. I would untie her and start looking around for Pedro, her boyfriend.
   c. I would untie her during the first commercial break—my favorite soap opera is on.

2. It's Saturday night, the club is packed. You're dancing like there's no tomorrow. Suddenly,

the music changes to a salsa song. What do you do?

    a. You get yourself a beer. You have no idea how to dance to this.

    b. You start shaking your hips like an epileptic. At least that's how you think salsa should be danced.

    c. You start grabbing and kissing all the women you can reach. At least that's what the Latino guys around you are doing.

3. A man lies on the street, covered in blood. A group of four attackers are still kicking and punching him, even when he looks unconscious. When they stop for a second, the man grabs an iron bar, stands up and knocks the four of them out. What is that?

    a. These are gangs. They are everywhere.

    b. It's a TV commercial developed to raise awareness about street violence.

    c. It's the Latino remake of *Iron Man.*

4. How do you answer if someone asks you something in Spanish?

    a. "Hey, buddy! Learn some English if you want to live here!"

    b. "Me sorry. I no habla ispaniol."

    c. You talk over him, also in Spanish, but louder.

5. You are watching a Latino soap opera on TV. One young and beautiful girl is crying. Why?

    a. I didn't know I had this channel.

    b. I have no idea. Now everybody is crying.

c. Easy. Maria has found her beloved husband making out with the blind maid while her disabled mother was dying in the other room.

Results:

0 to 5 points: You may think you are the PacMan, but you are one of the small dots that he eats. If your cable TV company offers a Latino package, you should get a lifetime subscription as soon as possible.

6 to 12 points: The media is always talking about the "middle American." I never knew to whom they were referring. Now I know it's you.

13 to 15 points: I'm really proud of both you and myself. I think some Latin American countries would be willing to grant you citizenship. However, keep in mind that your electric can opener doesn't work in Costa Rica without an adaptor.

PART 4
WORK AND POLITICS

CHAPTER 45

THE IMMIGRATION ISSUE

Don't get me wrong, we're not here to debate whether immigration laws are fair or not. The United States needs immigrants, that's an

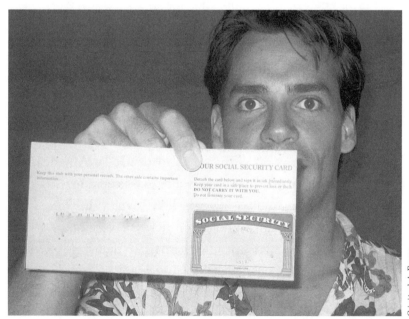

Cristián de la Fuente

Here I am with my brand-new Social Security number. You can't bend it, you can't laminate it, and you can't carry it with you. I don't understand. Why didn't they just send me the number and keep the card?

undeniable truth. It's a false myth the U.S. government doesn't want Latinos to come here. They just don't want *all of them*.

These days, you have to go through mountains of bureaucracy to obtain a visa. Immigration laws are getting tougher in order to discourage people who are doing so poorly in their own countries that they have nothing to lose and decide to leave. But what happens to the immigrants who could really make a difference in the growth of the country? They get tired. They're doing relatively well in their own country, so after years of being jerked around, they quit on their American dream. The U.S. government needs to do a better job advertising the benefits of the country to attract this kind of "qualified migration."

I'm willing to do my part for better Latino immigration in the twenty-first century. I've come up with some slogans designed to catch the attention of VIP Latinos and bring them to the United States. They will arrive by limousine and get the red carpet welcome. Here are the nominees:

- "America: same lifestyle, minus the gross social injustice."
  It's taxing (not literally!) to lead a luxurious lifestyle in a poor country, because everyone seems to think it's your fault there is no clean water to drink. In America, the poor just drink their clean water and keep quiet.
- "Come hang out with Salma Hayek and J. Lo!"
  In Latin American communities, everyone knows each other. They can't imagine it isn't like that in the United States.
- "Are you able to write and read? Apply for a visa!"
  Who are the only people who may get offended by this one? Illiterates. But how will they know what the sign says? *Exactly!*

CHAPTER 46

OUTSTANDING QUOTES FROM LATIN AMERICAN PRESIDENTS

Big truth: When it comes to political leaders, Latinos tend to have only short-term memories.

If you don't want to repeat your errors, you must remember them. To that end, I have compiled a number of remarkable quotes from famous Latin American leaders. The following are *quotes*. Hence, sadly, the leaders actually *said* these things.

- "I'm going to build in Venezuela a spaceship launching base."
  Hugo Chávez, President of Venezuela
- "Yes, I did a lot of pranks when I was a kid, and I'm still doing some as a president."
  Vicente Fox, President of Mexico
- "If they want to come here, so be it. I'm not afraid of that little prince."
  Leopoldo F. Galtieri, President of Argentina, daring the British fleet to sail south, which ultimately ended up becoming the Falklands War, where Argentina was defeated

- "History will absolve me."
  Dictator Fidel Castro, President of Cuba
- "Where there is hunger there is no hope."
  Luiz Inácio Lula da Silva, President of Brazil since 2003.
  The population below the poverty line in Brazil in 2005 was
  31 percent (based on "The World Factor" by the CIA)
- "I believe my skills to lead the country must be
  evaluated based on a thoughtful overview of all
  my time serving as a President."
  Alberto Fujimori, President of Peru between 1990 and
  2000, who resigned from the presidency by fax while self-
  exiled in Japan
- "I'm sorry, I've got the wrong speech."
  Carlos Menem, President of Argentina between 1989 and
  1999, after addressing the public for ten minutes from a
  piece of paper.
- "I'm not a dictator. It's just that I have a grumpy
  face."
  Augusto Pinochet, the military officer who deposed democratically elected president Salvador Allende to become
  president of Chile himself from 1973 until the return of
  democracy in 1990

I assume after reading these quotes, selected from among
thousands, you'll understand a little bit more why millions of
Latinos decide to try our luck in the United States.

CHAPTER 47

Latino Work Culture

Latinos are here to chase the American dream, and when we talk about achieving success in life, *working hard* are the key words. Some people say Latinos are lazy; others say exactly the opposite—that we work much harder than Anglos. So what is truth and what is myth? Well, the truth, perhaps, is that in our home countries, the work environment often leads to laziness. But in the States, most immigrants are determined to "make it" and will work incredibly long and hard hours. Let's look at the main myths one by one.

Myth #1: In Latin America, workers do the least that we can. This can be partly true. That doesn't mean we're lazy, don't get me wrong—we're more accurately labeled as "disappointed" than "relaxed." When the employers set aside the good jobs for their family and close friends, the pay is a mockery, the benefits a joke, and the chances to keep your family out of poverty are remote—if you have the strength to wake up and bust your behind after all that . . . you might have a martyr complex.

Myth #2: Latinos are always late to work.

The Latino's joyful character and desire to spread good cheer—and by this I mean to get his friends drunk—can be fatal to punctuality. It all depends on your point of view. Do Latinos stay up too late partying, or do businesses open way too early in the morning? In Latin America, even a modern office still has the punch-card clock you must use to prove your arrival time. There are countless cheats to hide a tardy arrival, from having your friend punch you in to buying your own clock and punching in while still at home. Who knows what we could accomplish if we didn't spend all of our time trying to outsmart the punch cards?

Myth #3: Latinos take more breaks at work than anybody else.

This is true. The reason is that in Latin America, there are not many chances to take a break. Most Latin American countries still allow smoking inside, so there goes the six ten-minute breaks U.S. smokers take in a day. An American worker might get coffee four times in a day, but this is because it's free. In Latin American countries, you have to pay, and you would break even buying that much coffee. Latinos have to be creative to get a break: fake a stomachache, get yourself locked in a bathroom stall, or jam up the copier really good. When you add this ingenuity to the already lax American employment culture, things can get out of hand. But let me ask you, what is a break? When workers remain at their desks, but they don't accomplish anything, is that not a break? When everyone receives a monthly paycheck, regardless of performance, individual effort is overlooked, and overtime is laughed at rather than recognized—who *isn't* on a break?

Myth #4: Latinos don't save money to retire.

This is true, but it's not because we spend all the hard-earned money on big trucks and trips to Disneyland. Most Latinos don't save money because we don't make enough to live on *today*. In Latin America, we stay at work—note that I didn't say "we work"—eight hours a day, six days a week, fifty weeks a year, for thirty-five years straight (if you're fortunate enough to not get fired or laid off). When the employee reaches his "golden age," his retirement check is not enough to put food on the table, which was the same problem he had when he was actually working. Are you starting to get why this Latino is happy to wait tables in the United States?

Myth #5: Latinos call in sick a lot.

That's true. I'm not ashamed. I know it's an excuse, but how do you think a person can manage to stay healthy earning the minimum wage? We can say: "Sorry, boss, I've caught a heavy cold, and I'm saving up for a bottle of Dimetapp, but until then, do you mind if I take off a little earlier today?"

Myth #6: Latinos don't want anybody to do our jobs when we are on vacation.

Of course we don't! "Oh, Luis went back to Mexico on vacation, but John is replacing him. He's doing such a great job! He doubles the results in half the time." Have you ever heard that? It happens.

While in most developed countries an employee tries to finish all of his pending work before going on vacation to ease his substitute's job, the Latino worker does exactly the opposite. Fifteen days before leaving, he starts to stockpile blank forms under his desk; a week before leaving, he erases some key files from his computer; three days before departure, he stamps "urgent" on every folder around, and he spends his last day at the office trying to find the best place to hide his desk drawer keys, especially for the drawers that have all the useful information the new guy will need.

A Latino worker will do anything to keep anybody from stealing his job. Losing that filthy position with the wretched salary, the daily abuse, and the bleak future—it's just unthinkable.

CHAPTER 48

Latinos in Politics—"Señor Presidente"

Truth #1: After the 2008 presidential election, the political arena has changed forever.

We are starting to witness a new era. If only I could travel back in time like Marty McFly, I would go back to the late 1890s. I'd find a freed black American slave, and I'd say to him, "Don't worry, in a little over a hundred years, this country will democratically elect a black president." He'd surely respond, "Go back where you came from, crazy demon! And take your pink typewriter with you!" It would've been that unimaginable. Seriously, it was that unimaginable ten years ago, but things change so fast these days.

Truth #2: Hispanics were one of the most sought-after voting groups in the 2008 election.

That was in part because we comprise about 9 percent of the eligible electorate. According to a nationwide survey conducted by the Pew Hispanic Center, five months before last year's election, Hispanic registered voters supported Obama over McCain

66 percent to 23 percent. So I think it's fair to say that the Latino community helped Barack Obama quite a bit to achieve his victory.

In 2008, when Latino activists took to the streets to protest against restrictive government policies on immigration, they carried signs that read: "Today we march, tomorrow we vote!" I would've added ". . . and soon we'll govern!" Will Obama's presidency open the door to a Latino immigrant president? What? Are you scared? Well, you should be.

Since Arnold Schwarzenegger was elected as governor of California in 2003, the issue of changing the Constitution to allow a non-U.S.-born citizen to run for the White House has become a serious topic in the media. I beg you—not as an author, nor as a voter, just as a nonnative U.S. citizen: Don't you dare allow it! If some immigrant believes he's so skilled a politician that he can fix a country, send him back to fix *his own* country.

LET'S GO TO THE "CASA BLANCA" (WHITE HOUSE).

Let's say someday Arnold pulls it off and gets the constitutional changes he needs. He'd run for president, and he'd lose, of course, because none of his movies had a monkey (I'm looking at you, Reagan). In the postelection press conference, he'd use his most popular catchphrase: "I'll be back." It's an empty promise, he won't run again. However—and this is the problem—he would've left the path open for other nonnative citizens to reach for the White House, and this time not just mopping the floor.

As soon as they say something's a crazy dream, a Latino will try to do it. As soon as they say a girl's single, a Latino will pat her butt. I'm 100 percent sure the next nonnative U.S. presidential candidate after Arnie would be Latino. If you thought 50 million immigrants in your country sounded bad, how about just one . . . with his finger on the button?

PRESIDENTIAL CAMPAIGN.

Antonio "Tony" Martinez is the Latino's dream candidate: mayor of Miami-Dade County at thirty-one, senator at thirty-five, governor of Florida at forty, candidate for the presidency today. Good image, great appeal, credibility, results, flawless behavior, role-model family. Truly American, except nonnative.

The campaign begins with month after month of touring the country, giving speeches, flying on a private jet, sharing his time, and sharing Bloody Marys with his all-female team: gorgeous press agent, publicist, stylist, speechwriter, and twelve other lovely ladies who make up his campaign committee. Sometimes, on the plane, they even have to all sleep together. I think that's why candidates always look so tired . . . because of the "hard work."

The campaign funding is going great. Tony Martinez's lifetime Latino friends—now rich and powerful entrepreneurs—are helping him. After all, most of them were part of the same street . . . "club" . . . twenty-five years ago.

He kisses a baby as soon as he steps off the plane, and he greets and thanks a war veteran—in a wheelchair would be great—before he gets into the limo. Once he's at the venue, he shakes hands with a poor woman who looks and smells like she came straight from her job at a fish-packing plant. The most important thing is to avoid a couple of common mistakes:

A. Don't confuse the names of the towns you visit.

B. Don't confuse the mayor's wife with the local groupies.

TV DEBATES.

As soon as the debate starts, Tony takes off his tie. He points his finger at his opponent and calls him names. An hour later, he loses the jacket. Some pundits wonder why he's so hot, but all the Latinos watching know what's going on—there's about to be a fistfight.

During a commercial break, one of Tony's advisors whispers that he should pretend to pass out as soon as they're back on the air. They'll blame it on campaign stress, and they'll avoid turning the debate into an Ultimate Fighting Championship cage match. On the one hand, people love a good fight; on the other, people also like to go to the circus, but that doesn't mean they'd elect a clown.

THE DAY OF THE ELECTION.

Finally the day has come. Everybody votes, including all of Latin America. Surprised? Not me—if an immigrant is allowed to run for president, why not allow his fellow compatriots to vote for him? If we look at it from a macroeconomic point of view, the U.S. president makes decisions that can have far-reaching effects all over Latin America. It wouldn't be right to deny them a voice in their own destiny.

When the votes are in, they're counted, recounted, and analyzed . . . and recounted again. And once again, just to be sure there's no error: Tony Martinez has become the first Latino immigrant president of the United States. But there *was* an error. There was an error indeed: bad constitutional amendments made fifty years ago, so that the Terminator could run for president. Now, it's too late to go back and fix it, even for a T-1000.

VIVA EL PRESIDENTE.

So much to do. To begin with, after months of endless celebrations, some vacation time and a brief visit to a specialized clinic to treat the new president's "exhaustion and dehydration." The "new" Martinez intends to be on top of things, especially certain ones that he thinks require urgent attention:

- **Redecorate the White House:** Where are the bright colors and exciting patterns: the reds, blues, yellows, greens, zebras, leopards, and florals? Let's spray-paint the furniture silver and get some flavor up in here! There should be a bronze statue of Che Guevara and a big gold crucifix in the Oval Office. How about a velvet painting of a sexy woman and her pet jaguar? Must the president think of everything himself?

- **Arrange a full upgrade of *Air Force One*:** So you're telling me we sent a probe to Mars, but we don't know how to put a Jacuzzi in a jet? Do you need NASA to show you how to hook up an Xbox?

- **Peruse all top secret files:** This is the real reason the president ran for office—to know the truth behind the Kennedy assassination, the "moon landing," and the Roswell UFO crash. After learning everything, the president will carry himself with a new smugness, a side glance, and an evil smile.

- **Action item:** Closing all borders to any kind of immigration. There are enough immigrants in this country. Some could call it "hypocrisy" or "treason against his own kind," but the president has his reasons: A Latino worker will do anything to keep anybody from stealing his job.

**TOP TEN THINGS YOU'D NEVER WANT TO HEAR A PRESIDENT SAY
(AND YOU PROBABLY WOULD IF THE PRESIDENT WAS LATINO):**

10. We're at war? Against whom?

9. Who wants a margarita?

8. Where is Iowa, exactly?

7. I have an idea for the economy—we'll sell tortillas!

6. How many people do I need for the cabinet? I have a lot of cousins!

5. The secretary of state is a *comemierda* (shit eater).

4. I can hold my breath longer than any other president.

3. How about I give you a million dollars and we both forget what you just witnessed.

2. What's this red button for?

1. What does it mean, "launching now"?

CHAPTER 49

Latinos Running the U.S. Economy

It hasn't happened . . . yet . . . but having gotten this far into the book, you should already have an idea of what could happen if this country's economy were controlled by Latinos. It's pretty obvious: It would soon start to resemble the economies of Latin America. What's less obvious: From whom could we ask for money?

Truth #1: An economist analyzes data, research, and market projections, and he makes logical decisions.

We Latinos like to let our hearts decide some stuff and also to add some "flavor" to everything we do. Applied to economics, it's like throwing a drunk into a shark tank and telling him to come back with sushi.

TOP FIVE MISTAKES OF A LATINO ECONOMIST:

5. Prices are going up? Let's raise everybody's salary.

4. Are we out of money? Let's print some more.

3. I know how to double the treasury—Vegas!

2. Vegas didn't work out . . . everyone get a second job.

1. Let's just default on these loans, what are they going to do—repossess the whole country? Where would they put it?

Big myth: If a Latino leads the U.S. economy, we would crash.

Is it true? Let's put together a possible scenario. First day, nine a.m.: nothing, because he doesn't make it to the office until ten fifteen. When he arrives, he sits down at his desk to check some data for the first time. Outside of the office, his underlings hear him yelling at the top of his lungs: "The national unemployment rate is six percent?!" They feel relieved, because it sounds like he's going to fix this country. What they don't suspect is that he's yelling out of happiness. For a Latin American economist, anything under 25 percent is good news: "This is just perfect, nobody touches anything, I'm going to play some golf." So if we did crash, it wouldn't be the result of anything our Latino economist did.

ANY GIVEN DAY IN A LATINO U.S. ECONOMIST'S LIFE.

10:45 a.m. Checks the unemployment rate and likes what he sees: it's under 25 percent.

11:10 a.m. Arrives at the golf course.

12:00 p.m. Lunch with Wall Street investors. They ask for

corporate handouts and tax cuts, having no idea the entire treasury was lost on the Dolphins-Patriots game. For some reason, they think that money is *theirs* to lose.

2:20 p.m. He comes back to his office and sees a top secret economic report lying on his desk. It's two hundred pages long.

2:30 p.m. The economist and a couple of friends make paper airplanes with the report and enjoy a few tequilas.

3:10 p.m. Meeting with the president. He wants answers.

3:20 p.m. The answer is: "I have no idea."

3:30 p.m. The president demands a plan before the end of the day.

3:31 p.m. The economist has a plan: to go to the movies with two lady friends and the president.

3:32 p.m. The president urges the economist to be careful. They both agree it's better if the girls come to the Oval Office instead of going out.

3:35 p.m. Press conference alongside the president. The subject: the U.S. economy's future.

3:40 p.m. The president introduces the Latino economist as the man in charge who'll explain the steps to follow.

7:45 p.m. The Latino economist ends his four-hour speech without offering a single tangible idea or solution, but everyone has learned about his hometown, his genealogy, his children's unique talents, the rivalries at his church, his grandparents' medical conditions, and his undefeated hot-dog-eating record at the county fair.

8:30 p.m. He stops by the White House with the two ladies. The president has given it a second thought and takes a
rain check on the date.

8:45 p.m. The economist has dinner with both ladies himself.
He explains to them the core principle of economics: whatever they demand, he'll supply.

Truth #2: Immigrants continue thinking as if we were still living
in our countries.
If a Latino assumed the responsibility of heading the economy
of the United States, the first thing he'd need is some time to
settle in: let's say six months. Don't worry, the economy would
surely look healthier without somebody running it . . . into the
ground or otherwise. However, that's not the problem. The crisis
will come when, sooner or later, that man will be forced to make
some decision or action, to show the rest of the country why he's
got the job. A laid-back Latino mind would run a capitalist and
industrialized economy with a whole new flavor.

- Down-to-earth
  Before making any decision, he'd want to know where
  we're standing—he'll visit the U.S. Department of the
  Treasury and ask to count the money, expecting a wad of
  bills folded in half, with a rubber band around it.
- New currency
  He'll change the dollar to a "peso gringo" and devaluate it
  245,000 percent, because he can't get used to the idea that
  a new car wouldn't cost 49 million pesos.
- Taxes on layaway
  From now on, the April 15 hard deadline for taxes is more
  like a guideline. Just pay them when you can, because we

know how it is. Just try to put something on it every month, like ten or twenty dollars.

• How much income tax should you pay?

Well, what do you have? If you have twelve goats, pay three goats. But if one of your goats is sick, just pay two goats . . . and don't try to give us the sick one!

• Disability checks

It's unfair to give monthly checks to certain disabled people, but not others. Newly recognized conditions shall include: hangovers, street-fight injuries, "crazy wife," and *empacho.*

• Better severance packages

Each employee who is fired will be granted an amount equal to two years' salary. If the employee stole from the company or sexually harassed the CEO's wife, he gets double for staying macho in such an effete society.

• The swan song

Finally, after all those mistakes, wrong decisions, and a profound economic crisis, the Latino economist would resign, explaining, "The world is changing. Our policies are not to blame for this crisis, but the global financial markets that sent our economy into a tailspin." As if China had suggested *mal de ojo* disability checks and the "peso gringo."

CHAPTER 50

Differences Between Anglos and Latinos, Part 4

The United States had some vacant positions, and those positions had the worst salaries in the country. Even though Latinos are doing the kind of work that no Anglo is willing to do, we are still happy about it. We want more, of course. We protest, but we are not planning on going back home, either. We came here for economic reasons, but we accidentally became—by our sheer numbers—a political force as well, which is how this country started in the first place: "no taxation without representation."

- *Situation A.* You meet with your boss to ask for a raise, and he denies it right off the bat.
  - **Anglo reaction:** You understand his key points.
  - **Latino reaction:** He understands his keyed car.
  - **Anglo reaction:** You take a personal half day to calm yourself down.
  - **Latino reaction:** You take $53 from petty cash to calm yourself down.

- **Anglo reaction:** You decide to shift your work into high gear and win your boss over.
- **Latino reaction:** You decide to shift your car into high gear and run your boss over.
- *Situation B.* For the first time, you are registered to vote. Now you have to pick who you are going with. How do you decide?
  - **Anglo voter:** Everything you need to know can be seen on candidates' Web sites.
  - **Latino voter:** Everything you need to know can be seen "in the eyes."
  - **Anglo voter:** You read the proposals from both parties on the economy, international policy, taxes, and health care.
  - **Latino voter:** You read your horoscope.
  - **Anglo voter:** At the end of the day, we need a good leader, regardless of political parties.
  - **Latino voter:** At the end of the election, you still don't know who the candidates are.
- *Situation C.* One day, you learn there is a rumor among your coworkers you may be homosexual, and that's not true. How do you state your position clearly?
  - **Anglo worker:** You start talking to every one of them individually about your sexual preferences.
  - **Latino worker:** You enter the cafeteria grabbing your crotch and shouting, "Where the bitches at?!"
  - **Anglo worker:** You ask your best friend if he can hook you up on a double date with the office hottie.
  - **Latino worker:** You hook up with the office hottie right at her desk.

- **Anglo worker:** You say to all of them: "May I have your attention? I'm not gay!"
- **Latino worker:** You say to all of them: "Every hour on the hour—until these rumors stop—I will reveal the name of one woman in this office I have slept with."
- *Situation D.* When a Latino husband and wife immigrated together, they didn't foresee the "land of the opportunities" could mean other romantic opportunities. Bottom line: they are getting a divorce. How that's different from an Anglo couple getting a divorce?
  - **Anglo divorcée says:** Our love is shattered.
  - **Latino divorcée says:** All our dishes are shattered.
  - **Anglo divorcée says:** We're going to be friends from now on.
  - **Latino divorcée says:** I'm doing his friends from now on.
- *Situation E.* As soon as the new president-elect takes office, the king of a remote land tells him they need to renegotiate all the economic treaties between both countries. What's the president's reaction?
  - **Anglo president:** He invites the king to come over to talk about the issue.
  - **Latino president:** He prank calls the king, insulting his mother and sisters.
  - **Anglo president:** He sends the U.S. ambassador with a gift from the citizens of America.
  - **Latino president:** He sends five aircraft carriers with a gift from the citizens of America.

- **Anglo president:** At the press of a button, my staff will set meetings, create proposals, and handle the situation.
- **Latino president:** At the press of a button, that guy's whole country is gone.

CHAPTER 51

So You're Anglo and Your Boss Is Latino . . .

This situation is unusual, that's for sure. Let's be honest, it's un-
common to see a Latino boss, and even less common to see an
Anglo under him. Although I did see it one time. I had this
meeting with the president of Fox Television Studios in Los Angeles so, as always, I prepared myself to meet an Anglo boss. I
entered the office, took a seat, and waited. A couple of minutes
later, a young Latino guy walked into the room and greeted me
in Spanish.

Him: "*Cristián, qué gusto conocerte, cómo estás?*" (Nice to meet
you, how you doing?)

I responded politely, and I thought that he must be the assistant, or the receptionist, or a Latino employee who recognized
me as a *novela* actor and stepped over to say hello. He then sits
in the president's chair. *Que huevos!* (How dare you!) If the boss
walks in right know, he will fire your ass, my friend! He just kept
on talking like he belonged in the chair . . . and in fact, he did.
He gave me his card, and I realized that a president of Fox was
Argentinean. I almost fainted when he introduced me to the vice

president . . . he was an Argentinean, too! I'm still waiting for their show proposal, by the way, so you know they didn't lose their roots.

Now I'd like address all the Anglo employees at Fox Television Studios. You're happily employed in a profitable company. Throughout the years, little by little, you've earned the respect and admiration of your fellow employees and bosses. It's the beginning of the year, the VP of Accounting position is available, and you know you're the natural candidate to be promoted. One Monday, you arrive at the office as you do every other day: eight a.m. sharp, well dressed, and in a good mood. You take a look at the VP office door and it has a name on it, *and it's not yours!* They've promoted somebody else, and nobody had the guts to tell you the bad news. The name is Jorge Lopez. You don't recall any Jorge Lopez, you don't know him, and he's not a current employee. Snooping around, you find out he's an expert in his field, recently arrived from the Dominican Republic, and he's going to be your new boss. You can't quit—you've spent your professional life there, plus you need the job. You realize that from now on, your chances to advance within the company rely on him, so you had better get along well with your new Latino boss. Let's get ready to rumble!

When you have a Latino boss, you are going to start noticing some changes in everyday life at the office. Instead of Muzak in the elevator, salsa and *bachata* will be played over the PA all day long—even though your division's business is the sale and distribution of Beethoven's masterpieces. The women will be encouraged—or failing that, required—to wear colorful miniskirts and tank tops instead of the mannish pantsuits of the past. Everything is reorganized, which you would describe as "messed up," and you think all this would make poor Beethoven roll over in his grave. The worst part is: Sales skyrocket. Jorge Lopez's changes are a complete success; meanwhile, you dropped Spanish class in high school like an idiot. If you hadn't switched to Japanese for an advantage in business, you'd actually have an advantage in business.

Another change you start noticing is the proliferation of Latino coworkers. The office is full of Garcias, Ramirezes, and Perezes. A lot of water cooler conversations are in Spanish, and the Dominicans form an unbeatable company baseball team named the Beejovenes. The cafeteria has *aguacate* and chicken with rice; gone are the hot dogs and macaroni and cheese. One thing is clear: These changes are here to stay, and you have two choices— adapt or perish.

THE FIVE COMMANDMENTS TO WIN OVER YOUR LATINO BOSS:

1. *Thou shalt learn Spanish.* Study it on your lunch break at your desk, so everyone can see. If your boss walks by, ask him for some translation help— this will let him know your commitment to bilingualism and also provide bonus face time. Note: Make sure your boss *knows* Spanish. He might have arrived here at age three and never learned a single word of it.

2. *Thou shalt ask a lot of questions.* Latinos love to talk, even on subjects we don't have a clue about. Make him feel important. Even if you have a Ph.D. in classical music, ask him, "Hey, boss, what's a sonata?" When he answers something like, "It sounds like it comes from *sonarse*, to blow one's nose, so it probably has to do with trumpets," just smile and thank him for his wisdom.

3. *Thou shalt fit on your desk as many pictures of your family as you can.* Latinos have a strong bond with our families, and at work, we like to show we are family people. We carry in our wallets photos of every blood relative, living or dead. We show them to anybody, and we also expect to see other people's photos. Do you want a raise? Show your boss that you are exactly like him, and you will get that promotion sooner than you think. If you are single, buy some magazines and cut out a model, some kids, and a dog, and frame them.

4. *Thou shalt laugh out loud.* It's very good to make your boss feel he's in the spotlight. If he tells a joke, you burst out in laughter—it's as simple as that. If he makes a joke about Anglos, go ahead and guffaw. That'll show your boss you're not up-tight. You should also laugh when he shares a joke in Spanish—just make sure he's actually telling a joke and not disclosing the amount the company's stock is down.

5. *Thou shalt invite your boss over for dinner.* For Latinos, gathering at the table is an intimate moment. In order to establish a healthy professional relationship with your Latino boss, there's nothing better than a delicious homemade meal fixed by your wife to honor him, a non-office-related conversation, and an effort at getting to know him better. Let your wife know she should make a lot of food, because chances are your boss will show up with his wife, six children, a cousin from

Michigan, and his mother-in-law. He'll also ask for the leftovers, whether or not he has any pets.

TOP FIVE THINGS YOU SHOULD NEVER SAY TO YOUR LATINO BOSS:

5. I tried to call you yesterday, but you always leave the office so early.

4. What happened to your eye, are you in a gang?

3. No, I'm afraid "casual Friday" doesn't have anything to do with sex.

2. Isn't it against the fire code to have your mother frying bananas in your office?

1. I'm not saying you're not a great boss, you are—but you still can't take my wife out on a date.

CHAPTER 52

So You're Invited to Dinner at Your Latino Coworker's House ...

It is not New Year's Eve. It's just another Latino dinner reunion with some friends. And believe it or not, we are not drunk. Latinos don't need to be drunk to get crazy. We're born crazy.

245

Some companies have these ridiculous "teamwork" policies, which include a bunch of useless phrases like "There's no I in team." Well, there's a "me" in team, what about that? These meetings last forever, there's a lot of talking in circles, a lot of coffee, and a lot of boredom. Sooner or later, every teamwork exercise unveils a harsh truth: Coworkers are completely incompatible. As if all this wasn't enough, your Latino colleague, Jacinto Perez, comes up with the great idea of having an out-of-the-office meeting. He invites everybody over to his house next Friday night with the sole purpose of reviewing all the teamwork ideas in a more personal environment. Your boss loves the idea. There's no way to escape—next Friday night, you'll meet Jacinto at his house.

THE ARRIVAL TIME.

Latinos are always late by definition. If we say eight o'clock sharp, we don't want to see you before 9:45. Now, what happens when the event is in our home? Are we late then, too? Hell, yes. If you arrive at 8:15, nobody will be home. There's a famous case—a man named Jonathan Waynebrow was invited to dinner at his Latino friend's house at 6:00. Jonathan didn't just fail to wait until the implied 7:45 arrival time, he actually showed up at 5:50! Not only was his friend not there, the house was still under construction (the workmen were also Latinos).

WHAT TO BRING?

Showing up empty-handed would be very rude. A bottle of wine is a classic gift, yet this is going to be a business dinner. Alcohol doesn't seem to suit the meeting—unless you wish for Jacinto Perez to get drunk and stab your boss, of course. A little present for each member of the host's family isn't a good idea, either. Remember, it's a Latino family, so four cousins could have shown up this morning, and it would be awkward to have gifts for everyone except them. The best option is something for the house, something uniquely American. How about a framed collection of limited-edition commemorative quarters—like the fifty states—at $12.50? It's valuable without being expensive, tasteful, simple, not too big, and no one could call it pretentious.

THE IMPORTANCE OF THE FIRST IMPRESSION.

After you've waited forty-five minutes at his door, your host returns home and greets you. Within the security of your comfort zone—the conference room—you feel confident about a nod and a "good morning." Outside the office, you're not so sure; you go in for a friendly handshake, but your Latino host gives you a bear hug that lifts you off the ground. Since you're at his house, you've become a friend and a brother, instantly.

Next, you must greet Jacinto's wife. Ninety-nine percent of the time, Latinos and Latinas greet by kissing each other on the cheek. If you don't kiss Jacinto's wife, you could be considered cold and distant. If you do kiss his wife, you could be considered an opportunistic gringo. The best you can do is keep your eyes open and read her body language when her husband introduces you. If her body remains rigid, she doesn't want to be kissed; if she leans forward and turns her head, she does want to be kissed; if she jumps into your arms and gives you tongue, she wants a divorce.

ETIQUETTE RULES.

All the guests are there, ready to have dinner together. Before we continue, let's highlight the events from 6:00 p.m. until now.

5:45 p.m. You and the rest of the Anglos arrive at Jacinto Perez's house.

6:30 p.m. The door opens, and you go in. Introductions begin.

7:15 p.m. You finish greeting all the family members in the house.

7:30 p.m. They start a round of cocktails to loosen everybody up.

7:45 p.m. Somebody vomits in the living room, but it's not a drunk coworker—it's the host's nine-year-old son, who has acid reflux condition.

8:15 p.m. The host arrives and greets everyone.

8:30 p.m. Everybody sits at the table, ready to eat. The host asks for a minute to fix himself a cocktail.

9:00 p.m. Dinner begins.

You've never experienced so many flavors, smells, textures, colors, or quantities of food on one single table, and this is just the appetizer. Everybody agrees to leave the business talk for later, so they can enjoy the meal. The host gulps down his drink, chews with his mouth open, guffaws, and speaks loudly—all at the same time. If you thought it was gross the way he spit all over you while talking in staff meetings, now it's not just saliva, but guacamole, hot sauce, and bread crumbs, as well.

Did you complain at the office about his animated body language and wild gestures? Well, now he is that much more dangerous, with a knife in one hand and a fork in the other, both of which he waves around while he speaks.

Dessert arrives, and Jacinto asks for a round of applause for his dedicated wife, who hand-made all the Mexican dishes served through the night. Everybody cheers for the cook—everyone except you, because you've been in the bathroom for the last fifteen minutes. Did you really believe that having Taco Bell twice a month was enough digestive training to get you through tonight?

AFTER DINNER.

Your time in the bathroom has taken longer than you planned, since trying to "eliminate signs" was really a challenge. While sitting on the throne you rehearsed presenting your fresh business ideas. You've been doing your homework and working hard for days to prepare for this meeting. When you finally come out, you discover your presentation will have to wait a little bit longer, since Latino meals are always followed by the *sobremesa,* a time to linger and talk over coffee or an after-dinner drink. It's 10:30 p.m. now, and all the guests look relaxed—maybe too relaxed— and the chitchat leans more to personal matters than business. They're all still drinking. This is the chronology of what happens after dinner:

10:35 p.m. Everybody moves to the living room for cocktails.

11:07 p.m. Williams, drunk, confesses to Jacinto he thinks his wife is a "hot pie."

11:08 p.m. There's a toast to Jacinto's wife.

11:15 p.m. The VP and the CEO of the company hug each other and begin singing "Yesterday."

11:22 p.m. Jacinto's nine-year-old son throws up again. This time, Williams joins him.

11:48 p.m. Shelly Kingsey, from Accounting, confesses she's a lesbian.

11:50 p.m. There's a toast to Shelly Kingsey.

11:55 p.m. There's a toast to Martina Navratilova.

11:58 p.m. There's a toast to Elton John.

12:11 a.m. Jacinto sends his son out to buy more alcohol, giving him the framed collection of limited-edition commemorative quarters to pay for it.

12:26 a.m. You start talking about your business ideas.

12:27 a.m. In the middle of your presentation, everyone agrees to a group hug to celebrate your creativity.

12:31 a.m. The group hug ends. They toast to you.

12:33 a.m. Jacinto's wife vanishes from the room. Both Williams and Shelly Kingsey follow her around the house making small talk.

12:51 a.m. The party is over. There's nothing left to drink.

12:52 a.m. Everybody says their good-byes, and there is much hugging and kissing, especially between Jacinto's wife and Shelly Kingsey, the accountant. Everybody cheers them on, even Jacinto.

12:58 a.m. Everybody's gone except for Williams and Kingsey, who have both asked to spend the night because "there are no taxis this late."

CHAPTER 53

So You Owe Money to a Latino . . .

The global economy has been undergoing a difficult period for approximately five hundred years. Add to this situation the fall of the stock market, the aftermath of 9/11, natural disasters, and skyrocketing insurance costs, and you are left with no corner to cut. "The American way of life" doesn't stop just because the money's gone, though. It's time to get a new credit card with a lower interest rate, transfer your balances, pay just the monthly minimum, get a second mortgage on the equity in your house, file for bankruptcy protection under Chapter 11—and any other chapter available—and, finally, when there's no other legal way to keep your lifestyle going, a friend of a friend recommends a "reliable" loan shark.

The main difference between a loan shark and a bank is bureaucracy. The main similarities are much more numerous:

- Both earn a killing on exorbitant interest rates.
- Both are eager to loan you more than you can repay.

- Both will ruin your life if you don't get them their money.

You've already called your friend and said how much you need, and an anonymous phone call confirms the time and place. That's it, done deal. You arrive ten minutes early, yet you can't find any sign of an office around. Not only that, everything seems to point to the fact that you're waiting beneath a highway. When you're about to leave, thinking this might have been a misunderstanding, a black limo followed by a black Hummer appears. They stop right next to you, the limo door opens, and a small alligator shoe steps out of the vehicle. A little man, wearing gold necklaces, gold rings, and a gold tooth approaches you and introduces himself: Danny Reyes, which means "Danny King." You shake his hand, and without saying another word, he gives you an envelope full of money. Danny smiles; he seems nice. He's Latino, but you don't care, business is business. You accept the money. The exact moment the envelope is in your hands, the light changes, dark clouds cover the sky, and thunder roars—all signs of a pact with the devil. Danny laughs in a sinister way that echoes all around.

There's no contract, no credit score review, not even "small print" you should read. Danny tells you: "The interest rate is seventy-eight percent, monthly, and we collect house to house. You don't have the money, we take a finger. You don't have fingers, we take a family member. Oh, I almost forgot, the loan started last week when I received the phone call asking for the money." Before you can open your mouth to complain, two of Danny's "executive associates" step out of the Hummer carrying a bag the size of a human body. Danny gives it a sideways glance and says: "We didn't have time to take out the trash." You nod while looking at your ten beautiful fingers. "This is a big mistake," you say to yourself, clutching the money.

Now you have cash and everything looks greener—except that sooner or later you'll have to confront Danny's men. One block away from home, a man cuts you off, rolls down his window, and says, "Danny wants to know what happened with his money." You reply the money is still in your pocket, since he gave it to you just fifteen minutes ago. You get the feeling Danny doesn't want his money back; he'd rather have your fingers.

You desperately try to figure some way out of your situation. The million-dollar question is: Is there any difference between being in debt to a Latino loan shark and one from a different background? Basically, all of them would be happy to cut you into slices if you miss even one payment, but you could have the upper hand with somebody like Danny "the King" Reyes if he has any of the following weaknesses:

1. You're friends with his cousin.

2. He's interested in your sister.

3. You're his immigration attorney.

4. You're a famous athlete on a team he likes.

5. You once saved his mother's life.

6. You're in a position to offer him a leading role in a *novela*.

I know what you're thinking, none of these will actually apply. It sounds crazy, but option number 5 is the only way out. You just have to follow Danny's mother for a couple of weeks and take note of her daily schedule. Get a friend to wait in his car in the supermarket parking lot, and when Danny's mother is coming back to her car, give your friend the signal. He should aim the car at Mrs. Reyes and slam on the accelerator—you, heroically, leap to her rescue, pushing her out of the way. When Danny hears the news about what you did, your debt will be forgiven, and you'll be safe again. Unfortunately, that's not going to be the case for your friend, the driver. Try to not pick a really close friend for this job.

I didn't want to close this topic without making something very clear: The issue is no different with a Latino acquaintance than with a Latino loan shark. We're the same, amateur as well as professional. The loan might be as innocent as a hundred dollars borrowed until next payday from Ramón Mendez, a colleague in the Human Resources Department of your company. Ramón wears sweater-vests and loves the opera, but if you haven't re-funded his money within two weeks, Ramón will break all of your fingers.

CHAPTER 54

So You Want to Get Rid of Us ...

Big Truth: As of today, there are probably about 60 million Latino souls living in the United States.
I have a lot of Anglo friends, and they've confessed to me they discuss the immigration issue at work on a regular basis—so long as Jose from the mailroom isn't around. They all say the same thing: Somebody has to come up with something soon, some kind of plan, before the situation can't be fixed. Maybe it's too late already. Although I wouldn't like to be labeled as a traitor to my own kind, I do have a couple of ideas that might work. I can't help it, I'm a problem solver by nature, and ideas just pop into my head.

Option #1: Develop a secret language.
Too many Latinos have mastered the English language. It's not the barrier to social and economic progress it once was. The plan would be that within five years, every Anglo living in the United States must use only this new language, and leave English to England. This will automatically prevent all Latinos from getting white-collar jobs, and it would also frustrate our economic

aspirations in this country. This plan is not a permanent solution, but it could buy another fifty years of Anglo domination.

Cristián de la Fuente

No, this is not me trying to cross the border. This picture was taken after I finished a scene from *Basic* in which I had just been shot by Samuel L. Jackson. I guess he too thought I was trying to cross the border.

Option #2: Return the favor.

The goal here is to move every Anglo—around 300 million people—to the Latin American countries, making them immigrants to the territories whose citizens originally migrated to the United States. Like most fun ideas, it's a short hop to the loony bin. Just imagine for a minute a fleet of the biggest, most magnificent U.S. Navy ships arriving at Cuba's shore. Nobody has a clue, the Cuban government is hopelessly awaiting an attack, people are running and screaming that it's the beginning of the Third World War . . . but then 9 million Anglo families dive into the water and swim toward the beach. They would infest the island like locusts, smoke all the cigars, and in just a few years, we'd surely see an Anglo fighting to change the Constitution to allow an American citizen to run for the Cuban presidency.

Option #3: Colonize the moon.

When in 1969 Lil' Frog stepped on the earth's lonely satellite, it was without a doubt a giant leap for mankind. Forty years later, it's time to put every U.S. citizen's feet there. Don't tell me that it's not possible. Technology has grown to levels beyond belief. My plan entails building a superstructured livable bubble, an encapsulated atmosphere big enough to hold 250 million habitants inside. It will be called the United States of the Moon. Obviously, to sneak illegally into outer space is harder than crossing a river. It will take a monumental effort, but the United States will finally be free of its immigration problems. Everything will be going great, except there are a few jobs no one wants to do: picking up moon rocks, cleaning the craters, and washing space dishes. At some point, someone's going to say, "Let's bring a spaceship full of Latinos from Earth, just a few." I don't think I have to tell you where this is headed.

CHAPTER 55

TEST #4—QUE SERÁ, SERÁ . . .

We're almost at the end of this journey, and whether or not you have a better understanding of Latinos, you've come this far, which proves that you *care*. You are a concerned citizen. You may be concerned that Latinos are taking over your country—but you are concerned nonetheless. The answers to this fourth and final test are not within the book, so in order to answer correctly, you must think outside of the box. At this point, you ought to have enough information to put yourself in a Latino state of mind: Enough said, "*Vaya con Dios!*" As always, give yourself 0 points for each "a," 1 point for each "b," and 3 points for each "c" answer.

1. You are applying for a credit card. They ask you for your Social Security number. What's the first thing that crosses your mind?
   a. You recite the number right away.
   b. Who are you, the police?
   c. What's a Social Security number?

2. The president has been caught cheating on his wife, what should we do?

   a. Throw him out of the office.

   b. Listen to him—if he regrets his actions, we can forgive him.

   c. We should gather in front of his house to applaud his *cojones*!

3. Yesterday, at the office, you lent a dollar to a colleague at the vending machines. Now it's almost five the next day, and he hasn't paid you back. What do you do?

   a. He'll pay you back tomorrow. No big deal.

   b. Ask him politely.

   c. Ask, "Do you play piano? You have such nice, delicate fingers."

4. You've been invited to have dinner at a coworker's house for the first time. What do you bring?

   a. A bottle of wine.

   b. A plant.

   c. A bag of empty Tupperware.

5. You are on your way to work. Your office is a couple of blocks away. Suddenly, a young and beautiful girl storms out of a building, furious. She looks you in the eye and says: "I just broke up with my boyfriend. I'm angry and horny. If you allow me, I will make all of your dirtiest dreams come true." What do you call that?

   a. An example of how decadent society has become.

b. A girl with some serious issues.

c. A good enough reason to get fired.

Ready for the twist? The scoring system is a little different this time. There are three options:

Option A: *You answered the four tests to the best of your knowledge. For real?* What are you, nuts? It was a joke. I'm an actor from Chile, not a therapist. You are definitely an Anglo citizen who lives life "by the book" (no pun intended), but you have to learn to read between the lines, at least if you want to adapt to the changes coming in this country.

Option B: *You flipped through the book, looking for specific topics you were interested in. You read the tests but you didn't complete all of them.* This book is not a mystery novel that you have to read beginning to end to understand the story. You are *supposed* to flip through the book. Now, on the other hand, why are you such a lazy reader? Go back and focus on the parts that you skipped. I wrote them for your benefit, not for my health.

Option C: *You read the questions, enjoyed the funny answers, and understood they weren't real tests.* Aren't you a smartypants? Your know-it-all attitude doesn't help. Those tests contained some very serious and useful information, and you treated them like one big joke.

Now that you've read the three options, you must be confused. I started saying the tests weren't real, but I finished by telling you to find the information within them. How could that be possible? One doesn't cancel out the other; they just coexist as contradictions. The wisdom of it will come as our two cultures get closer and closer, like two tango dancers as their mojitos kick in.

CHAPTER 56

One Day Without Latinos in the United States

Let's be honest: You need us. Since we're just a few pages away from the end of the book, you ought to acknowledge it. It's one of your last chances, don't waste it. I'm amazed at the simple fact that even the government acknowledges this fact without saying it. Illegal immigrants are not supposed to be able to work, but someone hires them, so they become "illegal workers." In 1996, the Internal Revenue Service began issuing identification numbers to enable illegal immigrants who don't have Social Security numbers to file taxes. Is that not a double standard, wrapped in an irony, stuffed into a paradox?

Perhaps you live in a city with a low Latino population, and you don't see how your life would be different if this group of people hadn't migrated here. Even if you live in a ghost town or in the middle of a mountain, Latinos affect your everyday life. I'm not saying this out of pride; Latinos didn't *choose* to affect your life. They simply took the place somebody sooner or later had to take. If tomorrow all the Latinos disappeared from this country, another minority would immediately become "the largest minority," and it'd play the same role within society. Let's look at a traditional Anglo family who wakes up unaware that there's not a single Latino in their country anymore.

IN THE MORNING.

A mother is fixing her son and her daughter some breakfast in the kitchen. The father goes to the door looking for the newspaper. There's nothing there. The kids are late, so they eat their cereal, milk, and juice as fast as they can, kiss their parents goodbye, and run off.

Once the children are gone, the father complains about not having clean underwear in his drawer. His wife reminds him she couldn't do the laundry, since the washing machine is broken. The technician was supposed to stop by earlier that morning, but she hasn't heard a word from him. Half an hour later, the father leaves for the office—wearing yesterday's underwear. Heading out to the garage, he sees his children standing on the curb. The school bus didn't pick them up. The father has no option but to give them a ride.

Once in the car, he notices he's running out of gas, so he says he'll stop at a gas station. He's amazed that every single gas station they pass by is closed; no clerks showed up to open them. Luckily, there is enough gas to drop the kids at school and make it to the office.

Arriving at work, the man walks toward the entrance door intending to hand his ID to the security guard, as usual. Strangely, there's no one asking for it this morning. He thinks it's quite strange that nobody is watching the front door of the building, particularly because he works at a nuclear power plant.

He enters his office, and the first thing he notices is that his trash can hasn't been emptied, and the place smells like sour milk and banana peels. He dials the extension for facility maintenance, but nobody answers. He decides to keep focused on his own work and to forget about these details.

AROUND MIDDAY.

The mother, tired of waiting for the washing machine technician, and unable to reach anyone at the customer service phone number, resolves to get out and start her errands. She drives to the supermarket and gets her grocery list out of her purse. As she goes from aisle to aisle, she notices a shortage of most of the products. She begins to worry: Is there a hurricane heading toward us? What's going on?

The produce section is completely demolished. There's a lack of fruits, the floor is sticky, and they've run out of plastic bags. Once she has the few items on her list that were actually in stock, she pushes the cart to the cashiers section, only to find there is only one lane open and more than thirty people waiting in line before her. The problem seems to be not a single cashier showed up for work today, and the poor manager is behind the register trying futilely to cope with all the angry and impatient customers. People talk about some kind of epidemic flu that could have sickened all the employees at once.

Carrying the bags herself, the woman makes the long walk across the parking lot to her car. The young men who always helped her with the bags don't seem to be around. She loads the trunk and she's finally ready to go, but now the car won't start. She doesn't know a thing about cars, but she knows somebody who does. She uses her cell phone to call Tito's Automotive, a repair service that more than once got her out of trouble, but she gets the answering machine. It's hot, the sun pounds on the trunk where the perishable food is, there's not a soul around, and the car is dead. Evidently, it's going to be a long day.

ENTERING AFTERNOON.

The children go to the school cafeteria. The lunch ladies haven't shown up for work today, and there's nothing cooked. Not even the vending machines across the main corridor come in handy—nobody from the service company came to refill them. The boy gives up and heads to football practice. The lawn hasn't been mowed and nobody painted lines on the field. After practice, the team hits the showers. There are no towels, and no one refilled the soap dispensers.

The girl sings in the school chorus. Upon arrival, she learns everybody is waiting outside the auditorium because the door is still locked. Fifteen minutes later, Taylor, the baritone she's secretly in love with, has a brilliant idea and it involves her. It comes to his mind that the girl could sneak into the auditorium through a broken side window—she'd fit just perfectly—and then she'll be able to open the door from the inside. The girl says "yes" promptly to win over her beloved baritone.

Love's blind, which might be the reason the girl, while passing through the frame, gets a deep cut in the palm of her hand from a piece of glass. She accomplishes the task and opens the door, but that hand needs medical attention. The chorus director discovers what they've been up to, and he calls the school nurse's office, but nobody picks up the phone.

IN THE EVENING.

Although today's not been easy, the family always gathers together for dinner. The mother decided to leave the broken car at the supermarket parking lot, fully loaded with groceries, and to go back home on a bus. The bad news was she couldn't spot a single bus on the streets . . . and the taxis were sparse. "Is there a transport strike on top of everything? I must pay attention to the news," thought the woman on the long walk home.

At this point, the fantasy of a home-cooked meal seems almost utopian, so she calls to order a pizza delivery. A nice Italian chef answers the phone, but he informs her the delivery guy didn't show up today, so the best he can offer is takeout.

Right at that moment, the father opens the front door. He never found an open gas station, so he had to get a ride from a colleague. Where are the kids? The father was supposed to pick them up—given the vanishing school buses—but he totally forgot about the children, so he has to go out again. He rides his daughter's bicycle to the school and finds his filthy, sweaty son and wounded little girl waiting for him.

Heading back home once again, they pick up the pizzas and everything seems to be getting back on track, aside from the boy's smell and the girl's paleness, of course. Finally gathered, the four of them sit at the dinner table. Just as they are about to start eating . . . bam! Blackout. Total darkness. In their house, on the streets, around the whole neighborhood. The radio says the energy plant workmen didn't show up for their shifts, which led to a hazardous overheating, and the repair teams never showed up. The family tries to relax, take it easy, and laugh about it.

Because it's hot and the air-conditioning isn't running, the family decides to hang out in the front yard to catch some fresh air. As soon as they're outside, they smell a nauseating odor coming from the full garbage bags piled up at the curb. The waste truck didn't collect today, and the trash further spoiled in the heat. The little girl's wound starts bleeding again and she cries for help, her mother tries to help her but trips in the dark, the boy stinks to high heaven, and the father is getting a terrible jock itch from his recycled underwear. In the midst of this crying, complaining, sobbing, and chaos, the father raises his arms to the sky and shouts: "Please, God! Help me!" But he gets no answer. It seems God didn't show up for work today, either.

CONCLUSION

When you write a book and you reach the end, you have a mix of feelings:

1. Relief: "I made it. I have something to be remembered for."

2. Insecurity: "Now what will become of my pink laptop?"

3. Amazement: "What do you mean they are going to translate the book into Spanish? They make me write it in my second language only to translate it into my first language?!"

During several meetings with my editor and the people at the publishing house, in which they discussed the title, how the cover was going to look, as well as the promotion campaign, I found myself fantasizing about what will happen after the book is published. If it is a success, will many other Latinos in Hollywood try to write their own versions of the immigrant experience? That would be fine with me, as long as I get credit in the acknowledgments for doing it first. After reflecting a moment on my pioneer status, some questions popped into my head:

- Is the Latino community going to be mad at me?
- Is the Anglo community going to be mad at me?
- Who would bother to read a chapter called "Conclusion"?

I'm not going to say I'm a writer. I'm not that guy. I will say I really like attention—I'm definitely *that* guy. If you think about it, most actors at one point or another try to do something they are completely unqualified to do. It could be directing, making an album, or earning $25 million per movie. I don't have any interest in directing, I can't write music, and nobody is offering a fortune to have me in a film . . . yet. (Who knows? A lot of Hollywood blockbusters are based on books!) My point is, this book gave me the opportunity to express myself in a different and more personalized way. In many ways, acting and writing are similar activities:

- In both cases, you have no idea what you're signing on for.
- When you are on TV, everybody recognizes you on the street. When you carry your book on the subway, same thing—so long as your face is on the cover.
- An actor might hurt his arm on *Dancing with the Stars*. A writer might hurt his arm with carpal tunnel syndrome.

Am I going to write another book after this one? I don't know. It's up to you—how many copies did you buy? I might even be willing to give up my lucrative dancing career.

Now I'd like to be a little bit serious, at least in these last paragraphs. I hope that one day we don't see ourselves as Latinos, Americans, African Americans, Indian Americans, South American Americans, etc. I hope we stop finding more ways to separate ourselves, stop creating ethnic "neighborhoods" where only one kind of person is allowed to live. We live in a different world than previous generations experienced, and if we don't start working as a team, we will end up destroying it.

It's time to say good-bye. I really hope you enjoyed the ride. At the end of the day, all the truths and myths arrive at the same conclusion: Latinos are also Americans. We're from the southern part of the Americas, but from the same hemisphere, and from the same planet. We have the same dreams—dreams that you could relate to and understand, except they are in Spanish. On that note, please start your Spanish lessons as soon as possible. As a motivation, I will disallow my memoirs to be translated into English.

Un abrazo.

EPILOGUE

I know what many of you are thinking: *Where is the important part of the book? I mean, we all want to hear about* Dancing with the Stars.

Okay, I hear you, and your wish is my command. But before we can talk about what happened on *Dancing with the Stars*, we must begin at the beginning. How did I come to be the guy who was invited to be on *Dancing with the Stars* in the first place? Which is to say, how does one become this improbable creature: a Chilean actor living in the United States?

IT'S CALLED ACTING.

Since my youth, I've been acting in soap operas, which are the only prime-time shows we have in my country. We don't have the budget to do shows like *The Sopranos* or *24*. I've also been in some commercials and hosted TV shows in Chile. After a couple of starring roles, I was eager to expand my horizons, because for actors in Latin America, if you don't open new avenues once you start to become known, you soon start playing the "friend of the lead guy," then the "abandoned older brother," then the "returning father," and when they offer you "the paralyzed grandfather" (and you are only forty years old), you know that what they are really telling you is "Your career is over."

I decided I wanted to be in this business when I was a young boy in Chile. Somebody told me I was good-looking, so I went out and got some modeling gigs. Somebody told me I should be an actor, so I found some small roles that—with time—started to grow. Thank God nobody said I was an exceptional lawn mower. My life would be a lot different right now.

In order to get a job as an actor, you have to audition. This is like a job interview, except a job interview is usually a pleasant meeting with somebody who has something to offer, and an audition is a long and tedious process that crushes your dreams.

You might think, "How do you know where to go to audition? How do they advertise that kind of job? I never saw an ad in the newspaper." Exactly. Producers and directors don't want thousands of "nobodies" crowded outside their offices. If you are an actor and you want to know where the auditions are, you have to get yourself an agent. The tricky part is that agents don't want to represent an unknown actor, because they don't make any money. Therefore, how does an unknown actor get a job? If you read this book, then you know: you threaten the producer that's dating your sister!

COMING TO AMERICA.

A little more than ten years ago, I took a plane and came all the way to Hollywood to work on my first "American TV show" for a Hispanic TV network. It was shot in Tijuana, Mexico, and it was in Spanish—but it aired in the States! I didn't know it at the time, but that experience was extremely helpful. You see, I ate Mexican food, celebrated Mexican holidays, and became good friends with a lot of Mexicans. My driver, my cook, and my gar-

Cristián de la Fuente

I was shooting a series when I celebrated my first birthday in the United States. Production thought I was Mexican, so they sent me a Mariachi to sing *"Las mañanitas."* For Anglos, we are all Mexicans.

dener were Mexicans. Later on, I found out that Los Angeles works exactly the same way.

I started flying back and forth between Tijuana and Los Angeles, taking classes to improve my English (in Los Angeles), polishing my craft (in Tijuana), and enjoying the best margaritas (oddly, in Los Angeles). After one year and a lot of margaritas, I decided to move to L.A., mostly in order to save money on plane tickets. When I got my visa, I packed all my things. When Latinos pack, we travel with suitcases, bags, musical instruments (why would we leave the piano behind?), sixteen cousins who sleep in the garage, the car, our grandma's ashes, and hundreds of bottles of homemade medicine a neighbor gave us, whispering, "I warn you, trust no doctor there!"

Let me tell you this: It is completely and utterly different to arrive in the United States for a vacation—or for a short period of time—than it is to move there. Not only does it feel different, but they look at you in a different way. Until then, every time I

271

passed through airport security they always asked me, "How long are you going to stay?" A couple of weeks. "What are you going to do?" I'm promoting an upcoming soap opera in Spanish. "How much money do you have?" Not much, but they're going to pay me for this. "In case of an emergency, who should we contact?" An ambulance, please. They have this kind of look—if you are Anglo, I'm sure you've never noticed it—as if you were lying, trying to get through and stay in the country illegally until the end of time.

It was another story when I was finally moving to the United States for good. The security guys at the airport kept staring at me like "You finally made it" while they scrutinized my passport top to bottom. And the kind of questions they asked me were totally different than before: "Do you carry any plants, seeds, roots or animals with you?" I'm coming from Chile, not from the Amazonas. "Did somebody help you pack your bags?" Of course! All my family and neighbors gave me a hand. It would've taken me two weeks to do it by myself. Luckily, they laughed at that and let me go.

There are life experiences that you will remember forever. Your first kiss. Your first day at work. Your first kiss with a co-worker. Anyway, my point is that there are certain things that shocked me as soon as I was established in the United States, and they are as fresh in my mind today as when I tried to deal with them.

First, when I started living in L.A., I learned that in this country the standard way to refer to native citizens is "Americans," as if they were the only ones. Let's review the name of the continent south of North America: it's South *America*! Some Latinos challenge the use of the word "American" to denote U.S. nationals as arrogant and incorrect. I'm not that radical on the matter, I just say . . . share the word. I don't think U.S. nationals will ever say, "You know what? You are right! From now on, we're going to start calling ourselves *United Statesmen.*" Let's make a deal: it's not that we don't want you to call yourself Americans, it's that we'd like to be Americans as well, because *we are.*

The second shock I had was when I turned the TV on. I found out that they call a sport that's played throwing a ball with the hand "football," while another sport, widely considered to be the most popular in the world, where almost all of its players use their feet to kick the ball, is called "soccer." In addition, they have a beautiful name for the culmination of the baseball post-season, a championship series called the World Series. I was eager to see teams from Cuba, Dominican Republic, Venezuela, and Japan . . . but I was soon to discover that currently the only Major League Baseball team outside the United States is the Toronto Blue Jays, from Canada. Is it me or is that just too telling? "Americans," and in a small part Canadians, constitute the world? Of course, I still got to see the best Latino baseball players, because most of them are the stars of the "American" teams. Maybe that's the meaning of "World Series" after all. They hire the world's best players, but all the teams represent the United States. Baseball copies life; the difference is nobody complains about immigrants when they are winning the pennant for your team.

The third shock came when I first tried to call my family back in Chile, because of the telephone country calling code. If you are outside of the United States and want to call somebody here, the only thing you have to remember is to dial "1" before the actual number. Oddly enough, the United States shares that prefix with Canada (baseball, telephone codes, what are you guys up to?). However, when you are trying to call the rest of the world, you have to enter a combination of two or even three numbers that are very easy to get mixed up. Sometimes I find myself trying to make a call to Mexico (52) and I end up calling Chile (56), which my mom is always happy about, but that's not my point. My point is: How did the United States manage to keep the 1 prefix for themselves? The distribution of calling codes is based on a recommendation by the International Telecommunication Union, which has its headquarters in Switzerland. Even with their country hosting the organization, the Swiss couldn't do better than 41 for their prefix? Believe me, if Chile hosted the ITU headquarters, we would have gotten the number 1, but that's just how we Latinos are. If you want to top it all off, you have to dial 855 to make a call to Cambodia. I know what you are thinking: "Why would I need to memorize the prefix code of Cambodia? When am I going to use it or need it?" Hey, you never know, they might have some talented baseball players over there to star in our "World Series."

BIG HOLLYWOOD BREAK.

A couple of months after I was established in the United States, my Anglo friends gave *me* tips to survive as an immigrant. I remember some of them (and I never found them useful).

1. "Learn English, for real. This gypsy dialect that you try to articulate is useless."

2. "Pay your taxes in full and on time. I know it's a new concept for you, Cristián, but get used to it."

3. "Save for college. What do you mean you are not going to college?"

4. "This . . . is a credit card. What do you mean you have those in Latin America?"

5. "Give yourself some time to feel at home here. If you can't achieve that, go back to your country. Let's say . . . now."

Not only did I not speak English fluently as a new immigrant, I had no clue about the industry lingo. I thought living in Los Angeles would help me to practice the language, but I was wrong. It was "Spanglish" all over the place. The only thing I could do to improve my language skills was to watch TV. I'd go to sleep with David Letterman's show on. I didn't learn too much English, but I started organizing my life into "Top 10" lists, which was very helpful.

On a sunny afternoon around ten years ago, I went to my first audition in English. The room was full of aspiring actors, most of them Latinos. I wrote my name on a list and waited for my turn. The casting director entered the room, took the piece of paper, and started going back and forth looking at the list of names and at me. Then she said to her assistant, "We need a head shot of him." I panicked: "They are going to kill me!"

The assistant asked if I had a picture of my head. I thought, "They're not going to kill me, they want a picture to ask for a ransom!" As you can see, a Latino always lives in his own mental soap opera. Despite my fears, she skipped the other names to audition me first. She invited me to another room, and when I was ready to start reading my lines, she first wanted to know how I "saw the character" . . . in English. I can't recall exactly what I said; I don't think she understood half of it anyway, but as my mother always taught me: "If you can't convince them, confuse them." I started talking as fast as I could, I laughed, I raised my voice, I cried, and I cursed—and all that was just trying to say my name. At some point, she stopped me and asked for my "résumé." I had never heard of that word before. It sounded like the Spanish word *resumido,* which means "shorter," and I thought, "Cristián, you are talking too much. Just try to say your last name in English one more time and shut up." She had to show me three other résumés before I realized what she was talking about.

At the end of the day, she gave me the part. The Chilean guy, with no head shot or résumé, with almost no knowledge of the English language and an awful accent, got the job. The guys who were waiting outside probably thought it wasn't fair, but we all learned a valuable lesson on that sunny afternoon: There are no rules in the Hollywood jungle. In Latin America it's different. We have rules. Breaking them might be our national sport, but we have them. Since my first victory, I've been going to countless auditions, and I just want to assure you of one thing: they don't often have a happy ending. Auditioning is like buying a lotto ticket. In fact, sometimes winning the lotto is more feasible.

One time, my agent got me an audition for a role in an upcoming Robert Rodriguez project. He was already *Robert Rodriguez,* if you know what I mean. Has it ever occurred to you that "somebody" is "nobody" until he became "somebody"? My first agent always told me: "You are going to appear on Letterman when you have a name." I don't know if he wanted to rebaptize me or what. Robert Rodriguez had "a name," and when I auditioned for him, we barely talked. I read my part and, at the end, he said: "Interesting." I kind of figured I wasn't going to get it when, as I was in the middle of reading the part, he started playing the guitar.

I attended a lot of parties hoping to make industry connections, and at one of them I was introduced to Jimmy Smits. I started telling him how proud of him I was for carrying the Latino flag all around Hollywood. In rapid-fire Spanish, I explained my thoughts about how Latino actors should become a united force in the business. He nodded for about five minutes, then said, "I'm sorry, my Spanish is not good." At least he didn't start playing guitar.

When it comes to auditions, I have to say I've been on the other side of the table. I have my own production company in Chile, and we do casting sessions looking for new talent for our shows. Every time we do one, I pray to God for a little payback: an Anglo actor to show up.

> **Me:** "*¿Cómo te llamas?*" (What's your name?)
> **Him:** "My name's Gordon Felch."
> **Me:** *"No se entendió nada la huevá!"* (I'm sorry, come again?)
> **Him:** "Gordon Felch, I'm American, from Wisconsin."
> **Me:** "Well, I'm American from Latin *America*. Are you ready to read your lines?"
> **Him:** *"Sí."*
> **Me:** "What? Please watch your accent. I don't understand what you just said."
> **Him:** *"¿Sí?"*
> **Me:** [to my partner] *"Llama a los carabineros que se lleven a este huevón!"* (Call the police. I'm done with him!)

Within the entertainment industry, there's a lot of competition, and you have to be on top of your game every audition, every event, every day. You have to smile for every picture. You have to make a funny quip any time you have the opportunity. You have to talk, but never say something inappropriate. You have to love yourself and make others love you even more than you do. I could add that you have to be a talented actor to get a job, but both you and I know that's not true.

DANCING WITH THE STARS

If getting one television gig is that hard, getting two is almost impossible, right? Wrong. In this business, the more you work the more they call you, and usually they want you at the same time. What's more, the second gig takes place on the other end of the world. I honestly doubt it happens in other lines of work. Let's say this young girl finishes her education. She's a teacher now and she starts looking for a job. For about six months she goes to lots of interviews, but gets no offers. When she's ready to give up, she nails a gig as a fifth-grade teacher at Meade River School in Atqasuk, Alaska. She's so happy! She starts the following Monday, and that very night, when she gets back home, she finds her phone machine blinking. "You have one new message." Beep! "Hi, we are calling from John Love Elementary School in Jacksonville, Florida. We've heard great things about you and we'd like to offer you a position here. You don't have to leave Alaska—we'll fly you back and forth. Give us a call; we'd like you to start next week." Could you imagine?

The same thing happened to me the first time they approached me about participating on *Dancing with the Stars* (DWTS.) It was a couple of years ago, and I was shooting the first (and last) season of CBS's sitcom *The Class*, so I had to pass. A sitcom may be half an hour, but each episode takes four to five days to complete between script readings, rehearsals, and the actual shooting. Not that I had that many lines, but I really didn't have the time to meet with the producers of DWTS, which, by the way, runs on another network.

The Class was the main excuse not to do DWTS, but in reality I was afraid of having a whole country laughing at me. I decided to put all my effort into my character on *The Class*. Not only did I show up to every table reading with my lines memorized, I also did research for my character, I explored new territory in my acting classes, I worked with an accent coach; as I was finally getting comfortable with what I was doing, they canceled the show.

A couple of months after that, Deena Katz from DWTS called me again to see if I was interested. To my relief, I was already working in the first season of USA Network's series *In Plain Sight* and again I couldn't do it. I was still very frightened by the whole idea.

In December 2007, I was on vacation in Chile and Deena called me up a third time. I wasn't working, so I didn't have that excuse. I had to face my own demons, but first, I had a very long and thoughtful conversation with my wife. "Look, they want me in the show. I have to go back to Los Angeles to meet them. I'm so sorry to have to leave now, in the middle of our trip. I've turned them down two times, the least I can do is hear what they have to offer. I've been giving it a lot of thought, and I believe it could be a good step in my career. What do you think?"

"Oh," my wife said, "were you talking to me?"

"There is nobody else in the room."

"I'm sorry, I thought you were rehearsing for some role."

A few days later, I left Chile for L.A. On my way to the meeting, I tried to imagine what they were going to say. Most of my job interviews were for new shows or pilots. DWTS was entering its sixth season, and they had achieved massive recognition. They were an established ratings juggernaut. You couldn't appear on that show quietly, hoping nobody will notice.

I realized that the country I was afraid of was Chile. When you are born in a land where a man cannot have a pink computer, and if you still return to that country at least twice a year, how can you let them see you ballroom dancing on TV? If even gay Latinos are machos, what would this make me?

After the season premiere, everything was going better than

© Kelsey McNeal/ABC (American Broadcasting Companies, Inc.)

As you can see, the producers thought this would be an appropriate costume for a Latino dancer. The shirt and the pants are pink. If you ever go to any Latin American country, please don't dress in pink, unless you want to be asked out by a guy.

I expected (I wasn't kicked out). The whole season of the show was going to last ten weeks. On elimination day of week five, we found ourselves in the bottom two, against Priscilla Presley. I thought people would vote for her, because she is "a name." You have no idea how hard it is to be standing there, with that light over your head, waiting for the host to break the news to you. *Am I safe? Am I going home? Should I sell my pink computer to buy a plane ticket?* They pause, they milk the seconds for suspense. Sometimes you just have to control the desire to scream: "Please, Tom, read the damned cue card!"

Priscilla Presley, "the name," was eliminated that night. People all over the country voted for me, not just the Latino audience. It was a turning point. Something started growing in me. It was my blood, my ancestors, my culture making an ancient call: *You are in the competition and entering the second half of the season. We want you to win. We want you to go all the way. You can do it.* What? The same guy who wasn't sure he could dance at all a month ago was now dreaming of nothing less than the title? Yes, that's the way Latinos are wired.

I was more motivated than ever. I would dance for hours, nonstop, until I learned the choreography. On week six, we nailed the foxtrot and we received 27 points from the judges—our best score up to that point—to end in third place, after Kristi Yamaguchi and Mario. I knew I was going to be safe, and we sailed through week seven indeed.

I like to think that everything happens for a reason. Within the Latino world, we are trained to deal with adversity. A crisis is an everyday situation in Latin America. We rarely panic. We get used to troubled times, and that's no myth. The point is that radical changes are customary for Latinos. They happen all the time. I didn't know it back then, but I was about to be embraced by Latino fate that week. We were ready to dance the samba. Cheryl, my partner, trained me like an army general, so I was ready to go. Halfway through the number, I felt a pain in my arm that I couldn't bear. I injured my arm during that samba; the Latino rhythm that was supposed to help me achieve my big night was instead the moment I thought was the end.

Jason Merritt/Film Magic

Here I am after the elimination day of the seventh week, when I decided I wasn't going to quit the show.

The judges gave us scores based on our performance up to that point. After learning my scores, I was sent to the hospital to have my arm checked.

The diagnosis: Ruptured brachial biceps tendon.

The family term: He messed up his arm . . . *dancing*.

The feeling: They are all laughing at me, on national television.

That night was horrible. The pain, the embarrassment, the feeling that I left something unfinished kept torturing me all the way home. Then I was reminded of something that I always knew, but didn't think about very much—when somebody is in trouble, Latinos are the most supportive people in the world.

Kristy promised me I was going to be the first one to be photographed with the mirror-ball trophy. She kept her promise.

Everybody offered to give me a hand (no pun intended), and I got calls from my friends, from the friends of my friends, even from the friends of my enemies. I went to see a sports injury specialist, and we had this conversation:

Doctor: You have a rupture in your brachial biceps tendon.
Me: Am I going to die?
Doctor: Don't be dramatic.
Me: I did a lot of soap operas—
Doctor: You need surgery and you'll be fine.
Me: Will I ever play the guitar again?
Doctor: Like I've never heard that one?
Me: I'm sorry, I want your honest opinion. Do I have to quit *Dancing with the Stars?*
Doctor: Yes, of course.

Here we are on Disney's plane heading to New York to appear on *Good Morning America* after the finale of *Dancing with the Stars.* Although it was a fierce competition, we all celebrated together.

Me: I want a second opinion.
Doctor: You have no innate dancing ability whatsoever.
Me: Like I've never heard that one?
Doctor: Doesn't make it less true.

I was devastated. I couldn't find any doctor who would give me the correct diagnosis: keep competing on *Dancing with the Stars*. Did I give up? When you are Latino you learn that "no" really means "keep trying." It was the first show of week eight, and fifteen minutes before we went on the air, I was able to talk to Neal Elattrache, who is the best doctor in the world—and I'm moving my arm right now to prove it. He told me that I definitely needed surgery, but not necessarily right away. We could delay it three weeks, tops. That was all I needed to make it to the finals. Well . . . that, the Latino vote . . . and everybody else's vote.

I ran to the executive producer, who already had the show scripted around me leaving. The prompter was cued up with Tom's good-bye speech to me, and we were ten minutes away from going live on national TV, when I told him that I would like to remain in the competition, dancing with one arm only. He said that it was too late. I said that I understood completely, but if Tom asked me on camera if I was able to keep dancing, I was going to say *Yes*. I don't know what was going through his mind, but by his look I can imagine him thinking, "*Bloody hell!*" (He is British.) He finished his tea and crumpet and said, "Let me see what I can do, but I want the doctor's authorization in writing." The rest, as they say, is history. Not that schoolchildren will be tested on it, but just as a catchy phrase to end this paragraph.

Those last shows, I gave the performances of my life. We had to train harder than ever. Cheryl had to choreograph the numbers in a way that I was able to hide my injury and still have the dancing look smooth and natural at the same time. She did all of that with an amateur dancer like me as a partner. I didn't want to disappoint her, my wife, my friends, or my fans. I left my heart on that dance floor. I don't think the audience voted the way they did because they pitied me. I'm very proud of what we achieved, and I think *that* is what people noticed.

The very last show, I knew it was going to be almost impossible to win, but I would be lying if I told you I didn't hope to get that trophy. We were all aware that Kristi Yamaguchi was the most talented contestant from day one; she really deserved to be the winner.

Now everywhere I go, everybody asks me how my arm is doing, and they tell me that they voted for me—which is funny, because if everybody had really voted for me, I should have won. Maybe I should ask for a recount. More important, I think I proved that a Latino can make it big among today's mainstream TV audiences. By the way, the following season of the show, they didn't have a Latino star. I know what you're thinking: A Latino worker will do anything to keep anybody from stealing his job. But I swear, I didn't sabotage anything—it isn't my fault!